HARRY HOOVER

THIRD EDITION

MOVING TO CHARLOTTE

THE UN-TOURIST GUIDE

MOVING TO CHARLOTTE
THE UN-TOURIST GUIDE®
THIRD EDITION

Print ISBN: 978-0-9996478-4-4
Ebook ISBN: 978-0-9996478-3-7

CONTENTS

WHY CHARLOTTE?
FOREWORD

If you are an outgoing, positive, can-do type of person, I think you'll love calling Charlotte home.

Relocating families might tell you that they love the growing job market, low cost of living and four-season climate, or the range of neighborhoods from urban to rural, good public and private schools and universities.

Members of Charlotte's burgeoning creative class may tell you that they love the funky in-town neighborhoods like No-Da, live music venues like the Music Factory, Neighborhood Theater and the Double Door, our proximity to mountains and beaches and access to an amazing array of outdoor activities.

Retirees might mention our abundant churches, the highly-respected health care system, Charlotte's many museums and cultural opportunities, as well as one of the nation's best airports to get their grandchildren here for a visit.

Business owners would probably mention Charlotte's well-educated, productive workforce, our resilient, diversified economy, good transportation system, and our active Chamber of Commerce that helps integrate them into the Charlotte business scene.

All good reasons to be sure. As a native whose family has been here since 1751, my thoughts on why Charlotte is a great place to live may differ from the newcomer's. I love Charlotte for its people. The area was first settled by forward-thinking, optimistic, hard-working and welcoming folk. Religious and highly independent people with a charitable bent shaped this town and region. Their fingerprints remain on our collective souls.

If that describes you, then let's take a look at 11 more reasons why Charlotte might be for you.

#1. Four Seasons

Source: Brant Waldeck

Charlotte is known for its year-round clear, blue skies and bright sunshine. If you play golf, you'll discover you can play every month. Now, it's true that we have hot, humid summers, but the mild winters and the picture perfect springs and falls more than make up for that. You'll find the temperatures range from the low 30s to mid-50s in the winter, the mid-50s to the high 70s in the spring and fall, and the mid-70s to the high 90s in the summer. We typically have 109 clear days and 105 partly sunny days for a total of 214 days with sun annually.

#2. Trees

Source: Brant Waldeck

Newcomers and visitors often remark on our enviable green canopy of trees. American Forests named Charlotte one of the 10 Best Cities for Urban Forests in 2013. A drive through neighborhoods like Myers Park showcases the foresight of early 20th Century planners. City leaders continue that tradition today. There's a tough tree ordinance to help protect existing mature trees and ensure appropriate planting when new developments are approved. Through a public/private collaborative project called TreesCharlotte, we are planting a total of 500,000 trees—15,000 per year—toward reaching a long-term goal of 50% canopy in 2050. Additionally, the Charlotte Public Tree Fund, the Creek Releaf Program helps the reforestation of streamside buffers and the Big Tree Program to catalog and protect champion-sized trees.

#3. Low Cost of Living

You can live well here. Compared to the top 40 metro areas in the nation, Charlotte has the 15th lowest cost of living. Charlotte is 6 percent below the national cost of living average, much of that because Charlotte's housing costs are 17 percent lower than the national average. We have the 17th lowest residential property tax rates when compared to the largest city in each state. Our mild climate helps keep heating and cooling costs low. On top of that, our total cost of utilities is lower than the national average.

#4. Lifelong Learning

Source: Central Piedmont Community College

The hub of Charlotte's lifelong learning community is Central Piedmont Community College, or CPCC as we call it. Want to become an entrepreneur? Then, CPCC's Small Business Center is for you. CPCC also offers personal enrichment courses in dance, fitness, cooking, personal finance, self-defense, kayaking, even the history of Charlotte. The University of North Carolina Charlotte offers continuing education online ranging from accounting and healthcare to law and publishing, as well as certificate programs, and professional development courses. You'll find continuing education programs at other local universities, too.

#5. Excellent Healthcare

We hope you never need the expertise you'll find in Charlotte's top medical facilities. But if you do, you are in good hands. Carolinas Medical Center, part of Carolinas HealthCare System, is the largest research hospital in the region, and one of five teaching hospitals in the state. Novant Health is a North Carolina-based integrated healthcare system that serves 34 counties.

#6. The Great Outdoors

In an hour and a half you can be on the highest peaks east of the Rockies and in a little over three hours you can be basking on a beach. But outdoor recreation is abundant right here. Golfers will find more than 30 courses in Mecklenburg County alone. There are about 600 courses spread throughout the state. If water is your thing, the US

National Whitewater Center is home to one of the largest manmade rivers in the world. Ride the waves in a raft, or check out the ziplines and climbing wall. Of course, boaters and anglers will love the access to lakes, like Norman, Wylie and Mountain Island. Mecklenburg County is home to more than 200 parks and facilities on 17,600 acres of parkland. Charlotte also sports an emerald necklace of greenways, 37 miles of which is developed and another 150 miles is under development.

#7. Southern Hospitality

Charlotte is a city with both feet planted firmly in the New South, with the emphasis on "new". But we haven't forgotten our heritage of hospitality. When we ask you to come "sit a while," we mean it. Just look at the Charlotte airport next time you come through town. There are dozens of rockers turning the tree-filled Atrium into a big front porch. There are those trees again. We'll fill your glass repeatedly with sweet tea, share stories with you and maybe send you home with a foil-covered plate full of something sweet. When you move in, don't be surprised if a neighbor walks over before you finish unpacking.

#8. Homes. Sweet Homes.

Want to live uptown in a condo? Yes, you may. Turn of the century homes are available near center city, too. Check out the bungalows in Dilworth, or the homes in Plaza Midwood, a streetcar suburb begun in the 1920s. Myers Park and Eastover are excellent locations for uptown workers, if you have the money. But if you are in more of a resort living mood, you will find waterfront and water view options on Lake Norman, Lake Wylie or Mountain Island Lake. Our small towns host a variety of housing options, ranging from historic homes in Davidson to McMansions in Matthews. From extremely urban to rural, there is a home for you in the Charlotte region.

#9. Arts, Culture & Music

Charlotte is no New York, but it has an arts community many larger cities envy. Museums abound, ranging from the kids' science museum, Discovery Place to the Charlotte Museum of History, and from the Mint Museum to the Bechtler Museum of Modern Art. The

Blumenthal Center presents the best of Broadway and is home to 13 resident companies ranging from the Charlotte Symphony to the North Carolina Dance Theatre. Local actors earn their chops at places like the Actors' Theatre of Charlotte, Theatre Charlotte, and Children's Theatre of Charlotte, as well as in the smaller towns spread throughout the region. You can find music everywhere from acoustic performances in wine bars to national acts at the PNC Music Pavillion, and the Neighborhood Theatre.

#10. Can-Do Spirit

Source: Charlotte Mecklenburg Public Library Robinson-Spangler Carolina Room

From the time of the first European settlers to the region, Charlotte has been a town built on commerce and always looking for an advantage. Since Charlotte had no navigable river nearby, Surveyor Thomas Polk built his home in 1755 at the intersection of two Indian trading paths to take advantage of the commerce they promised. That crossroad today is Trade and Tryon—also known as The Square—

one of the busiest intersections in the state. The nation's first gold rush started in our region in 1799. Leaders successfully landed a US Mint for the purpose of minting coins, and this provided impetus for the later development of our banking industry. In 1849, Charlotte leaders saw the benefit rail could bring and fought to have the rail line from Salisbury extended to the Queen City to connect with the South Carolina rail system all the way to the port of Charleston. Charlotte put aside partisan differences in 2012 and successfully landed the Democratic National Convention. We understand that working together is good for business, good for Charlotteans.

#11. Giving Back

Our history of giving back starts with the church. Scots-Irish Presbyterians originally settled the area, establishing six churches spread widely throughout the county. In 1917, men at Second Presbyterian started the annual December luncheon of the Good Fellows Club to raise funds for the working poor. Today, there are 1,700 members who continue to gather in December, collecting money for those less fortunate. In 2012, the club raised more than $350,000 in eight minutes by cajoling attendees to write big checks. Their female counterpart group, Good Friends, raised another $156,000. Individual philanthropists have made their mark here, too. You'll see the name of Leon Levine, founder of Family Dollar, on facilities around Charlotte. He has donated millions to fund local universities, the Levine Children's Hospital and Levine Museum of the New South just to name a few. Since 1928, the Belk Foundation has led the way in charitable giving. The Belk Brothers founded a chain of department stores in 1888 and helped establish hundreds of rural churches near their stores. Later, their philanthropy turned to education and hospitals.

CHAPTER 1
A VERY BRIEF HISTORY OF CHARLOTTE

The Catawba—or people of the river—an offshoot of the Sioux tribe broke off and fled south to North Carolina around 1660 to evade their enemies. This tribe—the first known settlers to the region—lived along the broad estuary to the west of Charlotte, which became known as the Catawba.

Around 1740, the first colonists, primarily Scots-Irish and German, began to trundle down the Great Wagon Road from Pennsylvania into the Carolina back country. These self-sufficient folks began building churches, mostly Presbyterian, in the communities of Sugaw Creek, Rocky River, Poplar Tent, Steele Creek, Hopewell, Beatties Ford, Providence and Clear Creek.

Charlotte, NC Is Founded in 1769

To gain favor with the crown, local leaders named the settlement Charlotte Town and the county Mecklenburg in honor of King George III's wife, Charlotte of Mecklenburg-Strelitz. Queens College opened in 1771 to train young men for the ministry, but the king refused to grant the school's charter. More grievances against the king piled up. Charlotteans didn't hesitate to sign the Mecklenburg Declaration of Independence on May 20, 1775, a full year before the nation declared its independence.

Lord Cornwallis and his British troops swept into Charlotte in 1780, but stayed only about 10 days because the locals were so rebellious. He dubbed the place, "a hornet's nest of rebellion," a moniker we still proudly carry today. After the Revolutionary War, George Washington visited Charlotte and called it "a trifling place."

TRANSITION PERIOD: AVERAGE ROAD, 1898.

**Source: Charlotte Mecklenburg Public Library
Robinson-Spangler Carolina Room**

Events would soon begin to raise Charlotte's reputation. Though agriculture was still king, mining became important to the local economy. Iron ore was discovered and mined near the Catawba

River. Then, the nation's first gold rush began in the area in 1799, and Charlotte became the gold mining capital of the country until about 1860. The first branch of the US Mint was built here in 1836, producing more than $5,000,000 in coins during its service.

The Mint provided the impetus for North Carolina Bank and the Bank of Charlotte to set up shop here. No longer used as a mint by the 1860s, the building housed a Confederate hospital during most of the Civil War. Because of good rail connections with Norfolk, Charlotte became home to the Confederate Naval Yard in the last years of the war. Jefferson Davis, in full retreat, held the last meeting of the Confederate Cabinet in Charlotte, and it was here he learned of the assassination of Abraham Lincoln.

Even with transportation, mining and the advent of textile manufacturing, the population of the area remained relatively stagnant. In 1860, there were 17,374 people living in Mecklenburg County. It would be another 60 years before the Charlotte of today began to emerge.

Source: Charlotte Mecklenburg Public Library
Robinson-Spangler Carolina Room

A World War, A New Town

At the turn of the 20th Century, Charlotte's population was 18,091 and Mecklenburg's had grown to 55,268. In 1917, Mayor Frank McNinch managed to convince the federal government to place an Army training center in Charlotte. Camp Greene housed as many as 50,000 troops at a time. Many of these troops would return here to marry and settle down after their service in World War I.

Governor Cameron Morrison, a Charlotte native, was known as the good roads governor because of the web of roads he built, connecting every county seat and large town throughout the state. Charlotte, the geographic center of the Carolinas, benefitted from this network.

Source: Charlotte Mecklenburg Public Library Robinson-Spangler Carolina Room

The growth of so-called streetcar suburban neighborhoods, such as Myers Park, Elizabeth, Dilworth and Wilmore lured wealthy citizens out of the center city in the 1920s. Streetcars gave these residents easy access to their jobs uptown. You can still see some of the original streetcar stops today in Myers Park.

Charlotte's transportation infrastructure received a boost in World War II when the government dedicated an Army air base at Morris Field, not far from today's international airport, one of the busiest in the nation. In addition to the air base, Charlotte was home to a major Quartermaster Depot and a Navy shell loading plant.

After the war, the trifling place would become known as the Dixie Dynamo. Charlotte built the town's first single-purpose sports facility in 1955, the Charlotte Coliseum, which at the time was the world's largest free-span domed building. The town's population swelled to 200,000 by 1960.

But Charlotte suffered many of the growing pains common across the country. Returning veterans had moved out of town to the suburbs. Commerce followed, leaving the city center reeling from lack of business. Retailers followed the suburban crowds to the shopping centers that popped up around town, like Charlottetown Mall, the first enclosed shopping mall in the Southeast.

Bringing Uptown Back

Government and business banded together to successfully revitalize the center city. Much of their efforts focused on four down-at-the-heels center city neighborhoods, First Ward, Second Ward, Third

Ward and Fourth Ward. These got their names when they were split into political wards for election purposes in the 1850s. A 1993 public housing redevelopment project in First Ward—First Ward Place—received national acclaim, the light rail system was built and other commercial and residential development followed.

Second Ward, known originally as Brooklyn, was a busy urban area, home primarily to African-Americans. In the 1960s it was designated as a blighted area by the federal government and slated for urban renewal. Bulldozers leveled the area. The new Convention Center, where the 2012 Democratic National Convention was held, was built along the light rail line in Second Ward. The NASCAR Hall of Fame followed. Additional development, such as the construction of four Wells Fargo towers, has turned Second Ward into a refined business center. A plan calls for additional housing in the area, shops, restaurants and a high-tech high school.

Source: Charlotte Mecklenburg Public Library Robinson-Spangler Carolina Room

Third Ward was originally a mill village, but when the mill closed, the area became a streetcar suburb. The city added east/west connector streets in the 1960s, cutting up the neighborhood into smaller pieces. Bank of America's Gateway Village provided the spark for new development, and Third Ward has become the most diverse uptown neighborhood. Tailgaters rule Third Ward on game day at the nearby NFL Panther's Bank of America Stadium. You'll find the restored mill houses, new condos, uptown's only dog park, Wells Fargo Cultural Campus, and Johnson & Wales University. Also, the new Knight's AAA BB&T baseball stadium is being built there.

Historic Fourth Ward was where the city elite—doctors, merchants and ministers—lived in the 1800s. Streetcars lured wealthy residents to the suburbs and the beautiful Victorian homes began to deteriorate. In 1974, the Junior League began a push to restore Fourth Ward, one of the most desirable addresses in Charlotte today. Recent development includes a number of high rise condos, plus the NC Music Factory arts and entertainment complex.

Charlotte—no longer a trifling place—today is a bustling big city with small town charm.

CHAPTER 2

GETTING AROUND TOWN

For the purposes of this book, we'll focus on the City of Charlotte and Mecklenburg County, which form the hub of a 16-county metropolitan region that is the 22nd largest in the US. More than 800,000 reside in Charlotte and more than one million call Mecklenburg County home.

Our county is bordered by Iredell County to the north and to the south by York and Lancaster counties in South Carolina. Union and Cabarrus counties are to the east, and the Catawba River forms our western border with Lincoln and Gaston counties.

But first, let's be frank and discuss one of Charlotte's blemishes: transportation. All Charlotteans think we are NASCAR drivers, so we do not use our turn signals. Come on, do you really need them?

We have some other traffic quirks as well. We often change the names of roads for no apparent reason. You could be driving on Mulberry Church Road and then suddenly find yourself on Billy Graham Parkway. Next, it turns into Woodlawn, becomes Runnymede, jogs onto Sharon Road, becomes Wendover, and then it turns into Eastway Drive. I'm not making this up. That's confusing enough, but when you come to the intersection of Queens and Queens in Myers Park, you just want to park and walk. Luckily, we have some fairly decent interstates to get us around the confusion. Now, back to our geography.

North Mecklenburg

North Mecklenburg, historically a farming area, is generally considered to be the area from Sunset Road, northward to Lake Norman and Iredell County. In the late 50s Duke Energy built Lake Norman, which is the largest lake in the state, covering 50 square miles. It features 520 miles of shoreline, making it larger than the Sea of Galilee, and giving the area a resort feel.

Interstate-77, which runs the length of the county north to south, affords access to the lake and area towns Davidson, Cornelius and Huntersville. Highway 115 parallels I-77, while Highway 73 crosses the Lake Norman area from east to west.

Historic Davidson – population 11,750 – is home to Davidson College, both of which are named for Brigadier General William Lee Davidson, who died in a Revolutionary War battle. Presbyterians established the college in 1837, but it was not until 1891 that the town also took the name.

Contiguous to Davidson is the town of Cornelius, population 26,898, which was founded in 1893 and incorporated in 1905. The town was named for J.B. Cornelius, who although not a resident, provided the financing to build the cotton mill that spurred town growth.

Next door to Cornelius is Huntersville, the second largest municipality in Mecklenburg County with a population of 51,567. Originally named Craighead, the town incorporated in 1873 and took the name Huntersville in honor of cotton farmer Robert Boston Hunter.

Mountain Island Lake – the primary source of drinking water for the area—is also located in North Mecklenburg. You'll find the area near the lake dotted with historic sites, such as Latta Plantation, Rural Hill Farm, the Hugh Torrance House and Store, Alexandriana Historic Site and McIntyre Historic Site. Across from Latta Plantation is Hopewell Presbyterian Church, established in 1762 and still active today.

City of Charlotte

The city of Charlotte sits in the middle of the county circled by Interstate-485, its growth constrained in the north by Huntersville, in the south and southeast by Pineville, Matthews and Mint Hill. Charlotte's tentacles stretch beyond I-485 in some places to touch the county's borders.

From the northeast, Interstate 85 crosses our border with Cabarrus County, cutting west into Charlotte and meeting I-77 near center city before moving on to Gaston County. Interstate-277 forms a small loop around Uptown, encompassing the area south of the Brookshire Freeway, east of Independence Boulevard and Charlottetown Avenue, north of the John Belk Freeway and east of I-77. This is Charlotte's commercial heart containing the Convention Center, Carolina Panthers Stadium, the new BB&T baseball stadium, the NBA Bobcats' Arena, and many local, state and federal government facilities.

In a ring around the center city are urban neighborhoods such as NoDa (North Davidson), and streetcar suburbs like Plaza Midwood, Elizabeth, Myers Park, Eastover and Dilworth. Washington Heights, developed in 1910, was one of the nation's first streetcar suburbs aimed at middle-income black residents. The old industrial corridor that flanked Dilworth is inside the urban ring and now known as Historic Southend. A little further to the south is the toney SouthPark area, which is anchored by the prestigious shopping center of the same name.

To the west is the hard-working part of town, where many natives still live, and where you'll find Charlotte Douglas International Airport, as well as numerous government operations centers, such as Charlotte-Mecklenburg Schools' transportation center. If you are a pioneer, you might like FreemoreWest, a formerly downtrodden area that has seen the recent introduction of new housing developments and restaurants.

South Mecklenburg

Mecklenburg County's southwestern border abuts South Carolina, and its southeastern border is with Union County, NC.

The town of Pineville – population 8,236 – sits in the southwest corner of Mecklenburg, and features a number of small, local retailers and antique stores, as well as huge Carolina Place Mall. Pineville is the birthplace of James K. Polk, the 11th president of the United States. East of Pineville is Ballantyne Corporate Park, a 535-acre business development that features high end residential development as well as a golf course, spa and more than 40 restaurants.

Matthews and Mint Hill are situated to the southeast near our border with Union County, NC. Matthews was farm country in the 1800s, fueled by cotton and timber. When the railroad came through, the stop was named for Edward Watson Matthews, a director in the rail company. Incorporated in 1879, the town took the name that was on the old depot, which still sits in this bustling town of 30,008.

The Mint Hill community was first settled in 1750, but it was 1971 before the town was incorporated. Primarily a residential community, Mint Hill has grown to about 25,000 today.

Public Transportation

Charlotte is auto-centric, especially if you live outside center city. Would you really expect anything else from a town that has a NASCAR Hall of Fame? This is not the most bike friendly town you'll experience, nor is public transportation on the level you'll find in the large cities of the Northeast.

However, Charlotte Area Transit System (CATS), a network of light rail, trolleys and buses, is improving. LYNX Blue Line Light Rail connects the southern end of town with the museums, sporting events, and nightlife in the center city. Hybrid electric buses run from Charlotte Douglas International Airport into uptown every 20 minutes on weekdays and every 30 minutes nights and weekends.

Gold Rush rubber-wheeled trolleys offer free service along Trade and Tryon streets from 6:40 AM to 6:00 PM, Monday through Friday.

CATS' buses run more than 40 county-wide routes daily, providing service from 5:00 AM to 2:00 AM. Stops are well marked and fairly well distributed around town.

CHAPTER 3

CHARLOTTE'S WEATHER - MODERATION IN ALL SEASONS

Prior to writing this book, we conducted a survey of Charlotteans, asking what they liked and didn't like about Charlotte. Twenty percent ranked "weather" or "four seasons" as the best thing about the town.

Clear, Carolina blue skies and bright sunshine are a year-round hallmark of the weather here. Weather is a daily topic of conversation.

Keeping with the city's Presbyterian background, "moderate" best describes our weather. Our normal January maximum temperature is 51, while the minimum is 32. In June, the normal maximum is 87, with a 67 normal minimum. We get 43.5 inches of precipitation annually, which is less than Atlanta, Houston, New Orleans or Miami. Droughts are rare and Charlotte has never had a major flood.

Hurricanes and tornadoes are a rare occurrence here. North Carolina gets its share of tornadoes, but Charlotte—thankfully—is outside of tornado alley. Any hurricanes which make landfall on the North Carolina coast rarely affect us adversely.

Really, the only severe weather of consequence is the summer thunderstorm. Although North Carolina ranks sixth in lightning fatalities, Charlotte residents are more likely to suffer some lightning damage to their homes than to be injured. When you look at North Carolina lightning strike data, you see that Charlotte is near the middle of the pack. Just remember this safety slogan, and you'll reduce your risk: If you hear it, clear it. If you see it, flee it.

Welcoming Winters

If you like to shovel snow, you will not like Charlotte's winters. We average less than six inches of snow per year. But take my advice, stay off the roads on these rare days because most Charlotteans don't know how to drive in icy conditions.

When snow falls here, it typically sits around on the ground for a day, melts and then we move on with our lives. That's because only about half of our winter days see temperatures below freezing, which does help keep the heating bill down.

But when there is a threat of snow, or ice, we mob the grocery stores, buy every gallon of milk and loaf of bread available and then—to the bewilderment of northern transplants—we close the schools. It doesn't really make sense to buy a lot of snow removal equipment just to keep school open a couple of extra days per year.

Feeling the need for some snow? Charlotte is less than two hours from the highest peaks east of the Rockies and a host of ski resorts.

Sweet Spring

Our mercifully short winters are followed by a gradually warming spring. Average temperatures range from 51 in March to 68 in May. March is the rainiest month of the year, but it still averages 17 sunny days.

This is when Queen Charlotte dons her spring finery, beginning with ubiquitous dogwood trees and the redbuds in March. Other spring trees you'll see blooming include the Carolina cherry laurel and the wild black cherry. Dwarf azaleas dot home landscapes, and fragrant Carolina Jasmine climbs on many trellises. Keep an eye out—the Jasmine often blooms again in the fall.

As the temperature rises, festivals pop up everywhere, and the fish emerge from their winter torpor, spoiling for a fight. Spring rains raise the stream levels for kayakers and canoeists.

Sun- Kissed Summer

Yes, Charlotte can get hot and humid in the summer, but not as hot as some other southern cities. Jacksonville, Florida and Houston, Texas sport more than 80 days of 90 degree days each summer. Charlotte, on the other hand, averages only 40 days of 90 degrees.

Queen City summer temperatures average 76 degrees with an average daily temperature swing of 20 degrees. Cloud-dappled daytime skies and cool, clear evenings help keep the summer weather moderate. Our average relative humidity in the summer is 74 percent, which is lower than the 80 percent of the central interior of the US.

North Carolina's nearby mountains offer a cool respite if it gets too hot in Charlotte. Or, a three hour drive to the coast allows you to cool off in the surf.

Fabulous Fall

This is my favorite season in Charlotte. Summer temperatures moderate to an average of 72 in September, 61 in October and 51 in November. Cooler evenings bring fall colors to the trees, providing an autumn kaleidoscope rivaling that of New England. And the flowers of fall rival those of our spring.

Carolina blue skies seem to brighten every fall day, particularly in October, our sunniest month of the year. Fall, our driest season with an average of 10.85 inches of rain, offers you ample opportunity to enjoy a multitude of outdoor activities, including tailgating before college and professional football games.

Fall lasts well into November, easing you out of the summer doldrums and into the colder winter months.

So, weather is about the last thing you'll need to worry about here in Charlotte.

CHAPTER 4
LIVING HERE

In Charlotte, the living is easy—at least when compared to other similar sized markets. Our town consistently ranks among the most affordable in a comparison of the top 40 metro markets. In the second quarter 2013 listings, Charlotte ranked 12th most affordable market among the Top 40 metros, thanks to low costs on housing, grocery, health care and miscellaneous goods and services. Overall, the cost of living in Charlotte is 23% below the national average.

On The House

Although Charlotte home sales prices have increased dramatically in the past five years, they remain surprisingly affordable. In fact, the cost of housing has been hovering around 17% below the national average.

This is among the most affordable housing market of the top 50 US metropolitan areas with a median sales price of $227,000 in September 2017, a 7% increase from the previous September. In comparison, the national median sales price is $254,000. The median home listing price in Charlotte was $239,000 at the end of September 2017 according to Zillow. The median per square foot selling price stands at a reasonable $141 when compared to cities like Manhattan, NY($1759) Boston($621), and Washington, DC, $539).

Residences in the one- and four-bedroom size have seen recent price increases, while there has been some softness in the prices of two- and three-bedroom abodes.

HOME PRICE COMPARISON

Town	Median Sales Price	Avg. Listing Price
Charlotte	$184,500	$239,000
Cornelius	$267,000	$364,000
Davidson	$324,000	$345,000
Huntersville	$258,000	$275,000
Matthews	$221,000	$247,000
Pineville	$182,500	$202,778

Lakeside homes are more expensive, as are those in our many new gated communities with tons of amenities. There are dozens of golf course-centric neighborhoods, which also tend to be pricier. But even near the lake you can find a 1,383-square-foot, two-bedroom condo for $105,000. Plenty of well-maintained two and three-bedroom homes are available all over the county in nice neighborhoods for under $240,000. A 1,100-square-foot, two-bedroom uptown condo can be acquired for $320,000. Or, if you have the money and the inclination, pick up a 4000+ square-foot historic Eastover home for $1.5 million.

Compare Charlotte prices to others around the country:

- $599,000: A one-bedroom, 565-square-foot condo in downtown Boston

- $1,495,000: A 1366-square-foot condo in Beverly Hills, CA

- $719,000: A two-bedroom, 1342-square-foot condo in near North Chicago, IL

- $669,000: A one-bedroom, 785-square-foot condo in the Dupont Circle area of Washington, DC.

- $699,000: A three-bedroom, one bath 1100-square-foot condo in Manhasset, Long Island, NY

- $199,900: A one-bedroom, 475-square-foot condo in Washington, DC

- $249,000: A two-bedroom, 943-square-foot home built in 1949 in Miami, FL

Utilities

According to the most recent survey conducted by the Edison Electric Institute, North Carolina's average residential monthly bill for 1,000 kWh is $109, lower than the national average of $136. This is lower than the average bill in Virginia, South Carolina, Georgia, Alabama, Florida and Texas. The state's industrial average monthly bill of $29,000 also is among the lowest in the nation, well below the national average of $42,665.

Most local residents receive their power from Duke Energy, the nation's largest utility. Its estimated average monthly bill for 1,000 kWh is $102. A few areas around Lake Norman are served by the Energy United cooperative.

Natural gas service is offered primarily by Piedmont Natural Gas, the Southeast's second largest natural gas utility. Its average monthly bill is $55.92.

Water-Sewer

Most homes' water-sewer needs are served by the Charlotte-Mecklenburg Utility Department, or CMUD, as we refer to it. Mountain Island Lake on the Catawba River chain is the primary water source for our area. Several years ago a bond referendum was passed to buy watershed areas around the lake to help protect the quality of the water supply. In 2012, the EPA awarded CMUD with the Safe Drinking Water Act Excellence Award.

CMUD delivers safe and reliable water and sewer at very competitive rates. For example, 5,236 gallons(7Ccf) of water per month costs roughly $59 in Charlotte, while it would cost $82 in Charleston, SC, $84 in Chapel Hill, and $100 in Kansas City.

Telecom

More than 30 companies provide telecommunications services to Charlotte. There are more than 75,000 miles of fiber optic cable in Charlotte, giving customers access to a wide array of business and residential broadband data services.

AT&T, Time Warner Cable and Vonage are among the primary providers of voice over internet protocol services to the region.

Taxes

Individuals and businesses receive equitable tax treatment in this city and state. North Carolina corporate taxes are low and all firms are taxed equally, providing an even tax rate for all. Special tax rates are generally not allowed under North Carolina law. A study done for the Council on State Taxation found that North Carolina tied with Delaware and Oregon at having the lowest U.S. business tax burden. There is a reasonable business license tax levied by the city and county based upon the type of business and sales volume.

For individuals, the state income tax has been reduced to 5.75%, but there is not a local income tax. There is no state property tax. Locally, real property is assessed every four to eight years at fair market value. Personal property such as autos, trailers, boats and airplanes are assessed at the same tax rate as real property. In 2013, the combined Charlotte-Mecklenburg property tax rate was $1.30 per $100 valuation.

Charlotte has the 17th lowest residential property tax rates compared to the largest city in each of the 50 states. U.S. Census Bureau figures from 2008 reveal that the combined state and local per capita tax burden in North Carolina is 18th lowest in the nation at $3,591. The national average is $4,371.

Let's compare property taxes, based on 2011 rates, on the average home value in Charlotte of $316,140.

PROPERTY TAX COMPARISON

City, State	Assessed Value	Property Tax
Charlotte, NC	$316,400	$ 4,113.20
Jacksonville, FL	$316,400	$ 5,062.40
Houston, TX	$316,400	$ 7,973.28
Newark, NJ	$316,400	$ 8,226.40
Atlanta, GA	$316,400	$12,972.40
Columbus, OH	$316,400	$18,794.16

Source: Statistical Abstract of United States 2011

The Charlotte Chamber offers some excellent information on business and personal taxes.

How Safe Is Charlotte?

If Charlotte has another small blemish, it is in the area of safety. According to Neighborhoodscout.com, the crime rate in Charlotte is higher than the national average. However, for cities of similar size, Charlotte has a noticeably lower crime rate.

The chance of becoming a victim of a property or violent crime in Charlotte is 6.25%. There are 36.64 property crimes per 1,000 in Charlotte, and 6.22 violent crimes per 1,000 residents.

Police patrol the uptown business district heavily, so it is relatively safe. Overall, West Charlotte has the highest incidence of crime. On average, the neighborhoods get safer as you move away from the center city and into the small outlying towns, except for Pineville, which has one of the highest crime rates in America compared to communities of all sizes. Your chance of becoming a victim of a violent or property crime in Pineville is 13.5%.

The towns in North Mecklenburg have much better safety records. The crime rate in Davidson is lower than 80% of America's communities. Your chance of becoming a victim of crime is less than 1%.

Huntersville's crime rate is near the average of all communities in America. But compared to communities of a similar size, Huntersville's crime rate is noticeably lower. Your chance of becoming a victim is less than 2%.

The chance of becoming a victim of violent or property crime in Cornelius has dropped recently to 2%, giving it a crime rate considerably higher than the national average. When compared to cities its size, Cornelius is near the middle of the pack.

Mint Hill has a similar crime profile to Huntersville. Your chance of becoming a violent or property crime victim here is 1.8%, putting it near the middle of the pack for communities of all sizes. For cities its size, Mint Hill has a crime rate noticeably lower than average.

Matthews is more comparable to Cornelius. Its crime rate is higher than the national average, but about average when compared to cities of similar size. Your chance of becoming a victim of violent or property crime in Matthews is 3%.

If you choose your neighborhood carefully, you can cut your chances of becoming a crime victim. Neighborhoodscout.com features a crime comparison of neighborhoods and is a good resource as you are looking for a place to live.

World Class Healthcare

Charlotte's health care cost ranks sixth lowest among mid-sized U.S. cities. But it is not just the lower costs bringing people from all over seeking world class healthcare services in Mecklenburg County. Our medical professionals serve more than one million patients annually. Carolinas HealthCare System and Novant Health operate the major acute care hospitals here.

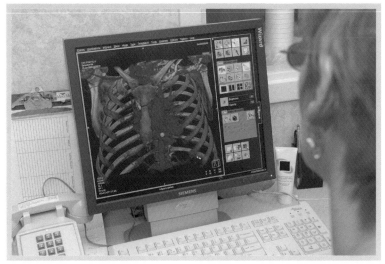

Source: Carolinas HealthCare System

Carolinas HealthCare System

Founded in 1940, Carolinas Healthcare is one of the country's largest not-for-profit, public systems. Headquartered in Charlotte, it has a network of 900 care locations across North and South Carolina that includes academic medical centers, hospitals, healthcare pavilions, physician practices, surgical and rehab facilities, home health agencies, nursing homes and hospice care.

Carolinas Healthcare's hospital network is called Carolinas Medical Center (CMC). There are eight CMC-operated hospitals in Charlotte alone. Since cancer and heart disease are the top causes of death in Mecklenburg County, you'll see that CMC has taken a particular interest in those diseases.

Nationally-known facilities include Levine Cancer Institute, Sanger Heart & Vascular Institute, Levine Children's Hospital, CMC Neurology, and The Transplant Center.

These facilities are strategically located in center city, in northeast Charlotte near the University, and in south Charlotte near Pineville. If you have a heart attack or are suffering from trauma, you want to be taken to CMC on Blythe Boulevard, where there are 80 heart specialists on staff. Additionally, it is North Carolina's official poison control center.

Levine Children's Hospital ranked among the US News top 50 children's hospitals in the nation for five specialties: cardiology & heart surgery, neonatology, nephrology, and orthopedics. CMC has won numerous other awards from J.D. Power, Blue Cross Blue Shield, the National Research Corporation and he American College of Surgeons Commission on Cancer.

CMC provides long term care and senior health services at facilities such as the Huntersville Oaks and Sardis Oaks.

Source: Carolinas HealthCare System

Novant Health

Novant is a not-for-profit health care system that primarily serves North Carolina's southern Piedmont region. It has five hospitals and a network of primary and specialty physicians.

The primary hospital facility in the Charlotte area is Novant Health Presbyterian Medical Center on Hawthorne Lane near center city. This facility—and its Novant Hemby Children's Hospital—is known for excellent nursing care. If you are pregnant, this is the hospital for you. Novant features a Women's Center dedicated solely to the needs of women and newborns.

Additionally, there are Novant hospitals in Huntersville and Matthews, as well as medical plazas in Ballantyne and in Steele Creek. Comprehensive primary medical care exclusively for older adults is provided by Novant Health Senior Healthcare, which offers homecare, rehabilitation and assisted living referrals.

Finding A Doctor

Source: Carolinas HealthCare System

Finding a doctor in a new community can be a daunting task. So, let's review some of your options.

If you find yourself in need of medical attention before you find a family doctor, you are in luck. There are a number of walk-in clinics, as well as many free and low cost clinics throughout the county, several run by the Mecklenburg County Health Department.

Uptown Express Care, operated by Carolinas HealthCare, offers walk-in services to those in center city. Novant Health provides a number of urgent care clinics in the Charlotte area. Many CVS Pharmacy locations feature a Minute Clinic for treating common, non-life threatening conditions.

Both Carolinas HealthCare and Novant Health feature networks of physicians. You can search for a physician through Carolinas Healthcare's find a doctor service, or via Novant Health's find a doctor service. Or, if you want a neutral third-party doctor finder, WebMD has a good one.

Another good local resource is one developed by *Charlotte Parent Magazine*. Its Mom-approved doctor list was compiled by surveying local moms. The list is searchable by zip code and practice area.

Concierge medical services are a relatively new idea, which typically provide on demand physician access for an annual retainer. Carolinas HealthCare has opened one called Perspective Health & Wellness. Signature Healthcare was the first medical concierge to open in Charlotte.

Other Health Care Resources

Community Blood Center of the Carolinas (CBCC) – an independent, non-profit blood center, is headquartered in Charlotte. It is the primary blood supplier for the region's hospitals. CBCC subscribes to a community-based banking philosophy, indicating that the blood given to the center stays in the community first to help family, friends and neighbors.

You can schedule an appointment to donate by calling 704-972-4700, or give at one of the many blood drives held throughout the community.

Hospice Care

Hospice & Palliative Care of the Charlotte Region (HPCCR) is your local resource for end of life care. HPCCR, operating since 1978, provides end-of-life services, ranging from hospice and palliative medicine to grief support and community education.

CHAPTER 5

CHOOSING WHERE TO LIVE

Charlotte is a housing market on the mend, which is good news for buyers. Housing prices suffered some major declines during the recession, with prices hitting bottom in January 2012, according to the National Association of Home Builders. Prices have grown more than 20% since the trough, but you can still find bargains in all types of housing. Another bit of good news: Charlotte's mild weather keeps homeowner's insurance low, as well.

Source: Gene McQueen for The Village at Southend

But it's not just about housing options, and there are plenty of those, ranging from high-rise condos, and townhomes to detached single family homes. Your challenge will be to determine your lifestyle options. Do you want a truly urban experience, a resort lifestyle, do you like golf or boating, want the privacy of a gated community, or do you want to get back to the land? You can have any of these options and just about everything in between.

Source: Gene McQueen for The Village at Southend

In our survey of Charlotte transplants, the top item they wished they'd had more information about when they arrived was the best neighborhoods. Of course, "best neighborhood" varies from person-to-person. We'll highlight a few areas that have fared well when it comes to maintaining property values, as well as those that have amenities many buyers seek.

Rent or Buy?

I often tell newcomers that they would be well-served to rent initially. There's plenty of short-term corporate housing available for this purpose. Renting lets you explore the region and determine what makes the most sense, particularly if you are moving here for a new job. Although the average commute is only 28 minutes, getting from home to office can be a pain if you live across town from work. Finally, if you have school-age children, this gives you time to figure out which neighborhood feeds which school. This can make a huge difference if your children are in the public school system.

Homes and apartments for longer-term rentals are in good supply. A number of new apartment communities have recently come online in Charlotte. You'll find some aimed at active adults, and some that are pet-friendly. Because of the increased supply, apartment rental prices are fairly reasonable.

You can do the legwork yourself if you want, using online resources such as craigslist.org, rental.com or charlotte.apartments.com. I recommend hiring a Realtor to assist you in finding your rental. They know the market, what is available, amenities of each community, and they can help guide you through the leasing agreement. This can be particularly helpful if you are renting from a homeowner.

Rents vary widely depending upon the neighborhood, the size of the rental, whether furnished, the length of the lease and other amenities. In the north end of the county, you often are able to rent a house for less than one of the newer apartments. Rents here range from $500 monthly for an older home to $2,300 for a luxury apartment in the master-planned community of Birkdale Village.

Apartments in center city run from $800 per month up to $6,587 at luxury developments like The Vue. In southwest Charlotte, the range for apartments is 545 to $1,700. Rental homes in this area are $1,295 and up. In south Charlotte, you are more likely to find an apartment or a condo than a home to rent. The range here is $690 – $1,800 monthly.

In east Charlotte, there is a wide range of rentals from student housing near the University for $550 per month to three bedroom homes in Mallard Creek for $1,425, and everything in between.

Finding Your Home

Around the fringes of the county and in our adjacent counties, you can still find larger undeveloped lots if you want to build your rural dream home. Along the western border, there are still lots available along the Catawba River. Also, there are dozens of new neighborhoods in which you can select a lot, a floor plan and build a new home, hiring one of Charlotte's many excellent homebuilders.

In center city new high rise condos compete with Victorian era homes, but currently the condos are winning. In First, Second, Third and Fourth Ward, you are most likely to find a condo for sale. Single-family detached homes come on the market less often here and builders are increasing the stock of condos constantly. Many professionals, and people with graduate level degrees, make the center city their home.

Light rail has driven mixed-use development in South End. You can find some older homes here, but most top the median price by a large margin. The condos available also tend toward the upper end of the market. South End is really more of a rental market. Apartments—most newly built—are abundant and varied. You'll find that a lot of younger people call South End home.

The streetcar suburbs of Dilworth, Elizabeth, Myers Park and Plaza Midwood make for easy commutes to uptown.

Dilworth is dominated by detached, single family homes built in the bungalow style. Homes there are in the $480,000 to $1.5 million range. Myers Park also has a high concentration of older homes, ranging from Tudors to bungalows. Myers Park Country Club helps boost prices into the $600,000 to $3 million range. Elizabeth features older homes as well, and you may find some around the $150,000 price point to as high as $800,000. Plaza Midwood is the most affordable of these near-uptown neighborhoods. You can find homes in the $350,000 to $500,000 range, while those that back up to Charlotte Country Club can top $1.5 million.

Eastover, dominated by red-brick Georgian revival style homes, was built in the 1920s and designed for commuters who owned automobiles. A few condo developments have sprung up on the edges of Eastover, and those are your most affordable options. Single family homes typically are in the $600,000 to $4 million range.

At the southern end of the county, new construction dominates, particularly around the Ballantyne Corporate Park and Ballantyne Country Club. There is a wide range of neighborhoods, featuring homes priced from $170,000 to $4 million.

In the southwestern part of the county is historic Steele Creek, the fastest growing region in Charlotte-Mecklenburg. This area is south of the airport, near Lake Wylie. In Steele Creek you can find condos in the $150,000 to $200,000 range and single family homes from $130,000 to $350,000. New master-planned neighborhoods such as Arysley and Berewick are very popular.

Lake Wylie straddles our border with South Carolina. You'll find plenty of waterfront and water view property along its 325 miles of shoreline. Huge Lake Wylie homes on multi-acre lots are available for those willing to spend $4 to $7 million. You can find homes in water access neighborhoods in the $200,000s.

Matthews, in southeast Mecklenburg County, features a wide variety of housing, from $140,000 condos to $2 million homes, most are in the $300,000s. In nearby Mint Hill, you can find older homes in the $150,000 range but the bulk of them are in the $250,000 – $350,000 range. You also can find properties classified as farms at $2 million and above.

In northeast Charlotte, you'll find University City, the high growth area named for the University of North Carolina Charlotte. Jobs in education, finance, insurance and high tech draw many professionals to this area. You can find many properties ranging in price from $80,000 to $250,000. Highland Creek is one of the more popular new neighborhoods in the area with homes there ranging from $175,000 to $500,000.

Mountain Island Lake is in an historic area northwest of Charlotte, where early settlers gathered for church at Hopewell Presbyterian, and where you'll find Latta Plantation, now a park and historic site. This is a much quieter lake than its larger sister lakes, Norman and Wylie. More than a dozen newer neighborhoods dot the area around the lake with homes ranging from $150,000 to $1 million for custom waterfront properties.

51

Lake Norman, with its eight public boat launches and 17 marinas, is a paradise for boaters and anglers. You can find all types of waterfront and water view homes, from custom homes in gated or golf course communities for the fulltime resident to smaller vacation type properties. You can find waterfront condos from $150,000 to sprawling custom homes upwards of $5 million.

Large lots and acreage, as well as small homes in the $150,000 range can be found on the outskirts of historic Davidson, and you can find condos ranging from the high $100,000s to the upper $300,000s. You can also find large homes for $1.5 million. The town's primary attraction is the older homes ringing the college of the same name. When one of these comes on the market, it is snapped up quickly.

There are still Huntersville building lots available starting at $19,000 up to 32-acre parcels for $2.7 million plus. Homes and condos range from $100,000 to waterfront homes in the $1.9 million range. Cornelius has a good stock of older homes for $200,000 to $250,000, with condos beginning in the low $100,000s. Custom waterfront homes here can reach $4 million and above.

Charlotte ... and Beyond

By Pat Riley

When I meet people and tell them I live and work in Charlotte, I'm surprised by the number who tell me they also know someone who lives here—or in many cases, nearby. That's the beauty of Charlotte—a vibrant urban core surrounded by lovely small towns, suburban communities, evolving neighborhoods and rural retreats.

Charlotte and Mecklenburg County is the center of a very diverse region of 16 counties, where you can find everything from auto racing to horse farms to lakes and town squares. While many of these counties are home to Charlotte commuters, most also stand strong on their own with growing populations, businesses and recreation options.

For example, more than 32,000 commuters come to Charlotte each day from York, Lancaster and Chester counties in nearby South Carolina. But these counties have also been highly attractive to relocating and expanding businesses because of their proximity to Charlotte.

If Charlotte is the hub, then delightful towns like Matthews, Shelby, Huntersville, Mount Holly and Mint Hill are the spokes of the wheel, each with their own character and sense of community. Davidson, Belmont and McAdenville are rich in history and charm. In Mooresville and Concord, you'll find the region's auto racing mecca—an economic engine in terms of both employment and enjoyment. In Union County, you'll find another kind of horsepower, with expansive horse farms in Weddington and Waxhaw. Lake Norman to the north and Lake Wylie to the south both fuel the region's power and water supply and provide abundant recreation options for residents and visitors.

Many settlers to this region came here from Pennsylvania, in covered wagons, bringing with them their own unique traditions and names for their settlements—Harrisburg, Lancaster, Chester and York. I was a modern-day settler (moving from Delaware and minus the wagon) in 1991. What I found here was a diverse home made up of all kinds of people, places and amenities. I was greeted by welcoming arms that invited me to jump in, get involved, and be a part. In the Charlotte region, no one is a stranger for long.

The front door to Charlotte is wide-open, with new college grads, mid-career professionals, busy families and retired grandparents flocking to the region. People move here for opportunity—jobs, climate, convenience to major transportation and overall quality of life. They find a progressive region where planning, growth and development benefit today and have been managed for the future. They put roots down in a place where you can see a Broadway play, shop in the newest stores, cheer on professional sports teams, attend a street fair or while away the day at a great fishing spot. Throughout the region, the wheels are turning.

Whether your mailing address says Charlotte, Gastonia, Indian Trail or Cornelius, feel free to tell people you live in Charlotte if you like. Because that's our approach—whatever makes you feel at home. All we ask is that you help us nurture and grow this special place, made up of people from so many other places that made the decision to make Charlotte home.

Pat Riley, president and CEO of the Allen Tate Companies, leads a team of more than 1,500 Realtors® and professional staff. In the past two decades, he has chaired the Charlotte Chamber, Charlotte Center City Partners, Arts and Science Council, Charlotte-Mecklenburg Public Schools Foundation and served in leadership roles for countless other community organizations. Riley and his wife, Robbin, live in Charlotte. He has three children and four grandchildren.

Finding A Realtor

A good real estate agent is essential. Agents know each community's eccentricities, amenities, as well as where the better schools are. They can help direct you to the neighborhoods that make the most sense for you. This cuts down on your legwork. You can just sit back and let the agent take you to see the most appropriate candidates.

How do you find a good realtor in Charlotte? Start with the list of agencies which led the way in 2016 transactions.

The *Charlotte Business Journal* reports that these are the top five firms in the Charlotte region based upon the number of transaction sides (sales in which a Realtor represented either the buyer or the seller) in 2016:

1. Allen Tate Companies   13,228

2. Re/Max Executive Realty   5,002

3. Wilkinson ERA Real Estate   4,131

4. Keller Williams Realty-Ballantyne Are   3,848

5. Keller Williams Realty-SouthPark   3,132

Here are the top five firms in terms of 2016 sales volume:

1. Allen Tate Companies $3.48 billion

2. Re/Max Executive Realty $1.3 billion

3. Keller Williams Realty-Ballantyne Area $1 billion

4. Wilkinson ERA Real Estate $998.23 million

5. Keller Williams Realty-Fort Mill $704.08 million

Or, you can search the Carolina Regional Realtors Association database of agents. There are many agents who focus solely on the buyers' market, and you can search only those by choosing "ABR – Accredited Buyer Representative" in the search form.

CHAPTER 6
SHOPPING

Grocery & Gourmet

Charlotteans don't lack options when it comes to groceries, and it seems the landscape changes every day in this competitive market.

Homegrown grocery chain Harris-Teeter is at the higher-end. Stores are clean, well-lighted, well-laid out and stocked. Founded in Charlotte in 1960, this 200-store chain operates in eight states and the District of Columbia. Kroger now owns Harris-Teeter but has not rebranded them. It features very high-quality store brands, and is known for its produce, bakery, and butcher shop, as well as chef-prepared meals. The Teeter, as we call it here, has excellent customer service. Can't find something on the shelf? Tell an associate and they will order it for you.

Since 1928 Reid's Fine Foods has operated from its Selwyn Avenue location, convenient to Myers Park, Eastover and the South Park area. It features a wide range of North Carolina products, like chocolate-covered peanuts and pecans, plus its own signature branded products. It is probably best known for its wine selection and prime grade meat, including bison, and grass-fed beef.

Florida-based Publix entered the market in 2013 to compete with Harris-Teeter, having already opened two stores across the border in South Carolina. They currently operate 14 stores in the Charlotte area. Like The Teeter, Publix is known for its clean stores, friendly staff, as well as its bakery.

Greensboro, NC-based The Fresh Market operates seven stores in our market. This chain's stores tend to be a little smaller, with a more intimate feel than Harris-Teeter or Publix. Warm lighting and classical music greet you when you enter. Meats and seafood all are behind refrigerated glass, not in plastic foam trays. You get to select the cut of meat you want. The Fresh Market features local, organic produce, 30 whole bean coffees from around the world, plus a bulk department with nuts, seeds, dried fruit, grains and spices.

Earth Fare, an Asheville, NC-based chain, operates three local groceries. It calls itself the healthy supermarket. Gluten-free options, organic and natural foods dominate the aisles. What you don't find in the store is more important than what you do. Earth Fare's philosophy is to offer products with no high fructose corn syrup, no artificial fats, colors, flavors, preservatives or sweeteners, and no antibiotics or bleached flour.

In the same healthy space as Earth Fare is Austin, Texas-based Whole Foods. This chain is focused on high quality, locally-produced organic foods like those from Carolina Classic Catfish and Eastern Carolina Organics. Whole Foods currently has two stores in the Charlotte market, one located in the South Park area and the other at I-77 Exit 25 in Huntersville.

California-based Trader Joe's, with its focus on value priced store brands, runs three stores in Charlotte. Trader Joe's stocks only about 4,000 items per store, roughly 80 percent of them are store branded. The store carries gourmet items, organic and vegetarian foods, as well as staples.

Salisbury, NC based Food Lion, at the value-end of the market, features aggressive promotions. You can find good deals on canned and boxed branded items, but I'd recommend finding your meat and produce elsewhere. Food Lion has 20 stores in Mecklenburg County, many of them older which need to be updated.

Charlotte Regional Farmers Market on Yorkmont Road near the airport is one of four state owned markets spread across the state. This is the largest local market, and one of the few open year-round. It provides local farmers a place to sell their fresh fruit, produce and meats, ranging from beef and pork to emu and ostrich. There is also a greenery shed where you can find flower, bedding plants, shrubs and trees.

Smaller farmers markets dot the Mecklenburg landscape. King's Drive Farmers Market, which has been open since 1941, is open Tuesday, Friday and Saturday and runs from April through October. This market is known for its assortment of North Carolina mountain apples.

In South End you'll find the Atherton Mill and Market, considered one of the nicer local markets. Other markets include:

- Matthews Community Farmers Market

- Center City Green Market

- Huntersville Farmers Market

- <u>Mecklenburg County Market</u>

Go Local

By Sara Crosland

Forget anything you've heard about ostentatious steakhouses or boring chain restaurants. These days, Charlotte's ever-evolving dining scene is brimming with savvy chefs, sleek restaurants, and locally grown fare from area farms.

**Source: Lisa Turnage
Taken at Atherton
Market**

If you're looking to get creative in your own kitchen, hit one of the city's urban markets like <u>7th Street Public Market</u>, which features stalls offering artisan cheeses, flavored salts, fresh-baked breads, or locally raised meats. Or stop in South End's <u>Atherton Mill and Market</u> for organic produce, locally made sweets, or fresh-roasted nuts.

There are also small shops around town offering innovative culinary options. There's fresh seafood at <u>Clean Catch Fish Market</u>, international spices at <u>Savory Spice Shop</u>, and house made chocolates at <u>Petit Phillippe</u>. The best part of these small stores though may be the people behind them. Full of cooking knowledge and creative ideas, you can't help but feel inspired after a chat over one of their counters.

For some serious inspiration though, make reservations at one of the city's inventive restaurants where chefs are creating dishes based on locally sourced cuisine. Stop in at <u>Halcyon Flavors</u> from the Earth, a chic uptown spot inside The Mint Museum of Art. Here, the Southern-meet-sophisticated menu features offerings like wild game, foraged mushrooms, and unexpected preparations of local produce. And plan on indulging in a cocktail with your meal here—the talented mixologist creates elixirs using Carolina spirits and seasonally inspired fruits and veggies.

If you enjoy a side of the see-and-be-seen scene with your dinner, stop in at 5 Church. This swanky spot's dishes like truffled shitake mushroom pierogies and seared sea scallops have made it a favorite among the culinary crowd, while its edgy ambiance (the entire text of *The Art of War* is scrawled on its ceiling) and specialty cocktails have cemented its title as top spot for the stylish set.

When it comes to offering consistently fantastic—and creative—dishes though, one of the city's best destinations isn't uptown. Soul Gastrolounge's location is part of its charm. Tucked on the second floor of an older building in the eclectic Plaza Midwood neighborhood, this cozy and convivial restaurant with exposed brick walls and lounge-like seating, has a menu packed with tasty small plates like sashimi tuna tacos, lamb lollipops, and foie gras cream puffs. Arrive early though because the secret is out on this spot and it fills up fast most evenings.

Luckily, if it is full, you can find plenty of other delicious offerings nearby. From small, ethnic spots to those classic upscale steakhouses, this city features dishes and destinations for a variety of palates. So make reservations or just stop in—and soak up the local scene.

Sarah Crosland lives in Charlotte and covers the city and region for numerous publications. The North Carolina native has been a lifestyle writer for almost a decade, but her first love has always been food. She authored the book Food Lovers' Guide to Charlotte *and her next book,* 100 Things to do in Charlotte Before You Die, *was published in 2014.*

Shopping Malls

Charlotte is covered with a strip malls, but has only a few higher end, enclosed malls.

But before we get to those high-end malls, you need to know about Park Road Shopping Center. When it opened at the corner of Woodlawn and Park Road in 1956, it was just a few feet outside of the city limits of Charlotte. Although the mix of tenants has changed some over the years, the mall still looks much as it did in the mid-20th century. A few of our favorites are Park Road Books, which has often been voted Charlotte's best bookstore, Blackhawk Hardware, and Sir Edmond Halley's pub.

SouthPark leads the way as the most upscale and has long been known as the place for fashion and style. Shoppers come from both Carolinas to visit this destination mall and its more than 150 stores, ranging from Apple and Burberry to Louis Vuitton and Tiffany. Women's apparel and jewelry stores are the big draw for SouthPark shoppers. Most major department stores have a presence here, including Belk, Dillards, Macy's, Neiman Marcus and Nordstrom.

For the younger shopper, Abercrombie & Fitch, Banana Republic, Gap and many others are located in the mall. Dilworth Coffee and Starbuck's keep you caffeinated, while Godiva Chocolatier and Haagen-Dazs feed your sweet tooth.

Dining options are plentiful-from the expansive food court to sit down restaurants like Cheesecake Factory, Maggiano's Little Italy, and McCormick & Schmick's.

Adjacent to the enclosed mall is The Village at SouthPark, where you will find Crate & Barrel, Paul Simon, Paul Simon for Women, as well as restaurants such as Cowfish Sushi Burger Bar.

Source: Simon Corp.

Carolina Place in Pineville with its more than 140 stores is also a destination for North and South Carolina shoppers in the middle market. Many of the same department stores you'll find at SouthPark—Belk, Macy's and Dillards—Carolina Place, as well as Sears and JC Penney. Stores providing children's apparel, toys and hobbies are abundant, as are service-related businesses such as Nail Spa and Oasis Massage. Trendy retailer H&M has recently opened a store in Carolina Place.

You'll find food in the well-stocked food court and at about every corner of the mall. Your choices include Asian offerings, plus well-known national brands like Auntie Anne's, Chipotle, Charleys, Sarku Japan, Sbarro, and and TCBY. Harper's, a locally owned sit-down restaurant is in the mall and several other restaurants, like Buca di Beppo, are on outparcels around the mall.

Just east of Mecklenburg County near Charlotte Motor Speedway awaits Concord Mills, North Carolina's most visited tourist attraction. Leave the heels at home and strap on your tennis shoes.

More than 200 manufacturer and retail outlets fill this huge, climate controlled, indoor mall. From Saks Fifth Avenue Off Fifth and Tommy Bahama to Ann Taylor Factory Store and Bass Pro Shops offer shoppers quite the variety. A lively food court and a 24-screen AMC theatre offer diversion when you have shopped until you dropped. There are many children's activities, including a go-kart track. A number of chain restaurants surround the mall, too, if you need to get away from the shopping for a while. Take my advice: unless you have the patience of Job, go on a weekday.

Source: Simon Corp.

Northlake Mall, as you might surmise from its name, is north of center city almost to Huntersville near the intersection of I-77 and I-485. It's a two-level, enclosed mall with more than 150 stores and restaurants, including five anchors: Belk, Dillard's, Macy's, Dick's Sporting Goods, and AMC Theatres. Retailers include Anthropologie, Pottery Barn, Brooks Brothers, Sephora, Fossil, Apple and Buckle. Grab a cup in the coffee court or a bite in the food court while junior checks out the Looney Tunes play area. There are sit-down restaurants attached to the mall, as well as a number of other restaurants surrounding it.

The latest thing is the village concept, where shopping, entertainment, dining and—sometimes—living are brought together as on small town Main Streets. Examples of these are Ballantyne Village, Birkdale Village, Blakeney, Morrison, and Phillips Place.

Other local favorite places to shop include Stonecrest at Piper Glen, Park Road Shopping Center, The Shoppes At University Place, Charlotte Premium Outlets, and the NoDa Arts District.

Hidden Gems

By Lauren Blake

Once you settle into Charlotte, you'll find plenty of opportunities to dress up: the opera, symphony and the many formal fundraisers for non-profits. You can hit the malls, of course, but there are many local boutiques where you might find something a little different to wear or to dress up your home.

Frock Shop (Plaza Midwood): Plaza Midwood has a reputation for catering to the quirky tastes of Charlotte. This unique shop does just that by satiating rare shopping habits with recycled fashion, vintage home goods, and local art in a restored Victorian home on Central Avenue. The shop is notorious for nodding to generations gone by while hosting frequent speakeasy parties celebrating the Roaring Twenties and famous literary characters. Once you step through the doors you'll feel like you travelled back in time. 901 Central Avenue.

Summerbird/Revolve (Dilworth): These charming shops share a refurbished bungalow in historic Dilworth that appeal to masculine and feminine tastes. Both offer sophisticated consignment, with labels ranging from everyday affordable looks to one-of-a-kind designer pieces that are hundreds of dollars cheaper than their retail counterparts. Summerbird offers women's designer dresses, blouses, coats, shoes and handbags as well as an impressive selection of local artwork and lighting fixtures. Revolve has similar finds for men, including professional attire, casual menswear and designer accessories like belts, watches and travel bags. 1222 East Blvd.

Capitol/Poole Shop (SouthPark): If you're seeking NYC worthy threads in the South, this is the retail gem to frequent. Featured in the *New York Times* and *Travel and Leisure*, these two upscale boutiques carry designer collections that you'd be hard pressed to find anywhere else in town or in the state for that matter. Poole Shop greets shoppers with envy-worthy labels that are amplified by the even more prestigious lines that Capitol houses. The "to be seen" locale often hosts designer trunk shows that give clients a sneak peak at new lines that are hot off the cloth. If your budget only allows for window-shopping, peruse the boutique's fashionably whimsical blog. 4010 Sharon Road.

Green with Envy: Your friends will be green with envy after you shop at this Plaza Midwood boutique. Inside the old Pet ice cream plant, you'll find clothing, gifts, home goods, and even items for baby here. This 4,000-square foot homage to shopping features the work of more than 60 Charlotte-area artisans. A huge assortment of wall art, pottery, glass, bath products, candles and handcrafted jewelry and handbags is on display. You'll also find handmade wooden kitchen accessories, even locally roasted coffee, and honey.1111 Central Avenue, #200.

KK Bloom (Selwyn): The enchantment of this shop is that it caters to women of all ages. Thus, it's the perfect locale to shop alongside daughter, mother and grandmother. From funky and youthful cocktail dresses to more conservative everyday-wear, there are a plethora of racks to sift through at this Selwyn shop. With an equal amount of accessory and jewelry lines, there's more to be found than just clothing. The colorful, and feminine, atmosphere entices girls and gals who want to have fun trying on options, while getting personal input from the young owner and employees of the shop. 2823 Selwyn Avenue.

Lauren Blake is a freelance lifestyle writer who contributes to local publications including South Park Magazine, Creative Loafing *and the nationally-acclaimed* Food Babe *blog. When she's not writing about craft cocktails, local businesses or organic living, she's typically enjoying one of the above, shopping or seeing live music. Blake lives in NoDa, where she is typically found writing at the local coffee shop, bicycling around the neighborhood or spending time with her beloved cats. She is a graduate of UNC Charlotte and holds degrees in Communication Studies and English.*

For The Kids

Charlotte, of course, has the usual suspects when it comes to kids clothing: Gap for Kids, Janie & Jack, Kid to Kid, and The Children's Place, for instance. But it also has a number of highly popular, locally owned shops. One of the most popular is Fancy Pants, a children's boutique offering upscale clothing from newborn to teen. A separate full-service kids' shoe store, Tootsies Too, is located inside Fancy Pants.

Menswear

Again, Charlotte features all the national menswear shops like Jos. A. Bank, Tom James Clothiers, and S&K Menswear. But, Charlotte, being such a banking town, has a number of high-end men's stores. Paul Simon, which also offers women's fashions, provides men with tailored clothing and formal wear, as well as sportswear. Another top-of-the-line store is Taylor, Richards & Conger.

On A Budget

There are a number of great used clothing stores in the Charlotte area, such as Plato's Closet, Buffalo Exchange, Sweet Repeats, Revolve Upscale Men's Consignment and Jilson's Men's Consignment. Nonprofits like Goodwill and the Salvation Army offer a number of locations in the area where you can find great bargains on gently used clothing.

A local favorite is the Charlotte Junior League Wearhouse. The Junior League, the nonprofit which operates the Wearhouse, was founded in 1926 by a group of women who wanted to assist local children and families in need. Proceeds from the Wearhouse help fund the group's charitable work.

Of course, Wal-Mart and Target are well represented.

Membership clubs are abundant for those who like to buy in bulk. There are two Costco stores in the Charlotte region.. Sam's Club has Charlotte stores in the University area, at Carolina Place, on Windsor Square Drive, in Pineville, in Matthews, and in nearby Kannapolis. BJ's Wholesale Club has stores in Concord, Mooresville and Pineville.

Furniture/Design

North Carolina, in case you don't know, is often called the Furniture Capital of the World. So, if you are looking for new furniture to fill your abode, you'll have plenty of options. Charlotte has some great furniture stores where you can find anything you need. However, I recommend that you travel about an hour northwest to Hickory, or an hour and a half northeast to High Point for the best selection and the best prices.

Shop the Hickory Furniture Mart, a four-level complex that offers a mix of factory outlets, custom showrooms and private galleries. You can find furniture here with prices up to 80% off retail, and you can shop here for accessories, indoor and outdoor lighting, oriental rugs and artwork.

High Point is the home of the International Furniture Market—the industry's largest trade show—because so many furniture manufacturers make their home in the area. The High Point Convention and Visitors Bureau is your source for furniture shopping information. You could easily spend a couple of days hitting all the retail stores and manufacturers' outlets.

If you find you'd like some interior design assistance, visit North Carolina Design Online for its directory of design experts, contractors and resources.

Charlotte has a number of excellent consignment stores where you can find used and even vintage furniture, if that is more to your liking. The Classic Attic in Park Road Shopping Center is a local favorite. Carolina Value Village Thrift Stores has locations in Charlotte and in the nearby towns of Kannapolis and Mooresville. Consignment First – with locations in Matthews and the University City area—often stocks closeout merchandise from the International Furniture Market.

67

If full contact garage sale shopping is more your style, you will have no trouble finding them. With our great weather, garage sales signs seem to be ubiquitous on Saturday mornings. You can find garage sale listings in *The Charlotte Observer* online classified section, and on Charlotte Craig's List.

CHAPTER 7
WHAT TO DO IN THE QUEEN CITY

Charlotte's calendar is always full of things to do, ranging from visual arts, the opera and theatre to the symphony, rock concerts and dance. Great restaurants, nightclubs, wine bars and craft beer breweries augment the cultural scene. Let's take a look at your available options.

The Arts Scene

Since 1958, the Arts & Science Council has raised funds for the arts community and has served as a clearinghouse for cultural events. Initially, the ASC supported only eight member organizations. Today, it supports artists, arts and cultural education, neighborhood cultural projects and more than 30 arts, science, history and heritage organizations, including Opera Carolina and the Charlotte Symphony.

Outdoor art is a hallmark of Charlotte's uptown. There are four statues, one on each corner at the Independence Square intersection, which represent commerce, industry, transportation and the future. But there is no better example of outdoor art than the Firebird, a sculpture that marks the entrance to the Bechtler Museum of Modern Art. Even the Bechtler building, designed by Swiss architect Mario Botta, is a work of art. The mid-20th Century collection includes works from Giacometti, Picasso, and Warhol to name but a few.

The Bechtler is a part of the campus known as the Levine Center for the Arts. This campus also includes the Uptown Mint Museum, Harvey B. Gantt Center for African-American Arts, and the John S.

and James L. Knight Theatre. The Knight, an intimate venue, hosts a variety of dance and music shows, ranging from the North Carolina Dance Theatre, the Nureyev State Ballet and Broadway plays to the Charlotte Symphony and bluesmen Buddy Guy and B.B. King.

Also uptown is the North Carolina Blumenthal Performing Arts Center with its three stages, where most of the Broadway shows are staged. The 700-seat McGlohon Theatre in nearby Spirit Square also has an occasional Broadway show. It is a showplace for live performances, including recent ones by Arturo Sandoval and the Tedeschi Trucks Band.

The Actor's Theatre of Charlotte, located a few blocks from center city, is home to a professional company dedicated to programming for mature audiences .

Source: Bechtler Museum of Modern Art

You have excellent opportunities to get involved with theatre if you have the acting bug. Theatre Charlotte is a non-professional venue which dates to 1927. Carolina Actors Studio Theatre in NoDa is also a volunteer driven organization. The Town of Davidson is home to the Davidson Community Players, where volunteers are always welcomed.

A few other uptown arts organizations include the Levine Museum of the New South, the Light Factory Museum of Photography and Film, and the McColl Center for Visual Art.

Away from center city are a number of other arts and culture venues. The Mint Museum off Randolph Road is located in what was the original branch of the U.S. Mint. Opened in 1936, it now houses the art of the ancient Americas, European and African art, as well as ceramics, decorative arts and fashion.

Source: The Mint Museum

The Charlotte Museum of History on Shamrock Drive features the Hezekiah Alexander House, the oldest surviving structure in Mecklenburg County. Wing Haven Gardens and bird sanctuary on Ridgewood Avenue is a great place for quiet contemplation, not to mention an outstanding venue for weddings.

Music lovers have a plethora of places to catch their favorite artists.

There's uptown's Time Warner Cable Arena. This is the home of Charlotte's NBA franchise, but it's also an excellent destination for top rated music acts like Eric Clapton, Michael Bublé, The Eagles, Jay-Z, and The Avett Brothers.

Or check out the NC Music Factory, a multiple venue arts and entertainment facility in Third Ward. Restaurants, bars and The Comedy Zone augment the musical venues like the Uptown

Amphitheatre, where acts ranging from Chickenfoot and Grace Potter to Steely Dan and the Jonas Brothers have performed. Next door to the amphitheater is an historic textile mill where you'll find the Fillmore Charlotte. It is themed in the tradition of San Francisco's legendary Fillmore.

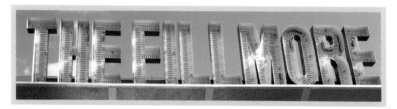

Near University City is the PNC Music Pavilionthat specializes in hosting large outdoor concerts. Jimmy Buffett brings his tour to perform for a crowd of Parrotheads here virtually every year. Many country music acts perform here, too.

Concerts often occur at the SouthPark Mall band shell. The Charlotte Symphony mounts the popular Summer Pops series here.

Craft Breweries

Delicious craft beers have found their way to Charlotte. And you can enjoy them in these local breweries.

Craft Tasting Room and Growler Shop	Bold Missy Brewery
Sugar Creek Brewing Company	Heist Brewery
The Unknown Brewing Company	Resident Culture Brewing
Sycamore Brewing	Catawba Brewing Company Charlotte
Birdsong Brewing Company	Hyde Brewing
Lenny Boy Brewing Company	NoDa Brewing Company
Three Spirits Brewery	Wooden Robot Brewery
The Olde Mecklenburg Brewery	Salud Cerveceria
Triple C Brewing Company	Free Range Brewing
Thirsty Nomad Brewing	Legion Brewing

Chow Down

Source: Queen City Q

One source reports that there are 3,270 restaurants and bars in the Charlotte region. Now, we won't lie to you—many of them are of the chain variety. But, not to worry, we can help you find the hidden gems tucked away around the city.

From vegetarian to carnivore, Asian to Cajun, and ethnic to homegrown, there is something for everyone. Let's start with the tried-and-true homegrown restaurants and work our way up to the high end.

Price's Chicken Coop in South End is your first stop. You stand in line, get your soul food and take it someplace else to eat. Bring cash—and don't forget the napkins. Next is Bar-B-Q King, a drive-in restaurant on Wilkinson Boulevard, which has appeared on Diners, Drive-Ins and Dives. As the name implies, they have barbecue, as well as fried chicken, good hamburgers, and a trout filet sandwich that has a lot of fans. Not far away from Bar-B-Q King is Pinky's Westside, where the White Trash Burger reigns supreme.

In Plaza Midwood, visit The Diamond, Dish, and Midwood Smokehouse.

Vegetarians can find plenty of options at Luna's Living Kitchen, the Woodlands, Carpe Diem and Fern. And, if you have other special dietary needs, such as gluten-free, try 300 East, Café Monte, and Dandelion Market. For the carnivore, go to Chima Brazilian Steakhouse, Del Frisco's and BLT Steak.

Italian fans must go to Vivace, one of my personal favorites. It has the best Italian wine list in town and features homemade limoncello. Fiamma and Luce are also good. Wan Fu is for the Chinese fan, while Yama Asian Fusion speaks to the Japanese lover. Viet-Thai Noodle House let's you get your Pho on.

Source: Applewood Gallery and Imaging – Johnson & Wales

10 TOP CHARLOTTE RESTAURANTS

1. The Fig Tree Restaurant
2. The Capital Grille
3. Viva Chicken
4. Carpe Diem Restaurant
5. Midwood Smokehouse
6. Bad Daddy's Burger Bar
7. The Cowfish Sushi Burger Bar
8. Pinky's Westside Grill
9. Mac's Speed Shop
10. McKoy's Smoke House and Saloon

Source: Trip Advisor

Now that you have finished your meal, what else is there to do? You can find live music virtually every night in Charlotte's clubs. Or, if you want to try out your own pipes, there are open mic nights at the Evening Muse, Smokey Joe's, Summit Coffee and Puckett's Farm Equipment.

The Queen City At Night

By Harry W Hoover III

Charlotte is full of nightlife entertainment highlighted by unique dining options, live music venues, nightclubs, bars and breweries. There are several distinct neighborhoods in Charlotte, each offering its own nightlife experience.

Uptown Charlotte, or center city, is the place to see and be seen. You'll find upscale dining options side-by-side with bars, breweries and nightclubs that are just around the corner from two—soon to be three—professional sports arenas.

The EPICENTRE in uptown Charlotte is a centrally located complex of almost 40 venues including restaurants, retail and late night spots. At EPICENTRE you can spend the evening bowling, watching the newest movie or eating dinner at one of the many upscale restaurants. Then, you can dance the night away in one of the nightclubs or sing your heart out at Howl At The Moon, the dueling piano bar.

The NoDa neighborhood, named for its location on North Davidson Street, is the historic arts district in the North end of Charlotte and is home to tattoo shops, friendly dive bars, art galleries and several local breweries, like Growler's Pourhouse. The arts are big in NoDa, so it is a fantastic place to hear live music from both local and major acts as well as browse several art galleries full of work from local artists. The Neighborhood Theatre draws artists ranging from funky Bootsy Collins to singer/songwriter Leon Russell. Or, head to The Evening Muse for open mic night.

NoDa also is the perfect place to people watch in Charlotte because it caters to such a broad audience of visitors. All of the bars, coffeehouses, restaurants and music venues are centrally located and easily within walking distance from one another as well.

Not far away, the Plaza Midwood area offers a more eclectic nightlife experience than most other Charlotte neighborhoods. From rooftop bars with skyline views to old school diners and from small local restaurants to global cuisine options, there is something for everyone here. Bistro La Bon has great carnivore food, but also has an excellent vegetarian and gluten-free menu. Roughly a mile northeast of uptown, you'll find trendy art galleries doubling as bars right next to punk rock bars, BBQ joints and farm-to-fork gastropubs, like The Peculiar Rabbit. This area is certainly the place for picky and adventurous eaters alike.

The Dilworth and nearby South End areas provide great places to grab a bite at one of the many pubs, to play pool at a billiards bar or to catch a game at one of the sports bars nearby.

The upscale South Park area just six miles south of uptown is definitely the place to enjoy a glass of wine and to spend an elegant evening in Charlotte. Several top-notch restaurants are located just outside the 1.6-million-square-foot mall and just around the corner from a number of wine rooms and tap houses. So put on your button-up or your little black dress and enjoy a swanky night in South Park.

Whether it's dinner in Plaza Midwood, beer in NoDa, wine in South Park or glitz and glamour in uptown, you'll certainly find a way to fill your evening in Charlotte.

Harry W Hoover III is the youngest child of native Charlotteans. After studying creative writing at North Carolina State University in Raleigh, Harry moved back home to Huntersville. He now lives in Charlotte where he puts his extensive hospitality background to use becoming a connoisseur of the cocktail.

The Sporting Life

Charlotte has a number of professional sports teams. The NFL Carolina Panthers play in the uptown Bank of America Stadium, while the Bobcats, our NBA franchise, play at Time Warner Cable Arena. Additionally, we have the Charlotte Hounds Lacrosse Team and the AHL Charlotte Checkers Hockey Club. A new uptown baseball stadium—BB&T Ballpark—opens in 2014 for the AAA Charlotte Knights. And there's Charlotte Motor Speedway, where NASCAR holds some of its biggest races. Area colleges field excellent teams in basketball, football and baseball, too.

Charlotte has a great network of YMCAs and an excellent park system with plenty of public fields and courts for those who would rather participate than just watch. Pickup basketball games and running groups can be found everywhere, and there's a solid martial arts community here, as well.

Fitness fanatics may want to look into F3 Nation, whose stated purpose is to plant, grow and serve small workout groups for the invigoration of male community leadership.

Golf is revered in Charlotte. You'll find at least 40 courses in Mecklenburg County, including Myers Park Golf Club, designed by famed architect Donald Ross. About 15 of the courses are open to the public, including five courses, a driving range and learning facility owned by Mecklenburg County Parks. Those include:

The Tradition – Prosperity Church Road, Charlotte

Cadillac Street Driving Range – Cadillac Street Pineville

Charles T. Myers Golf Course – Harrisburg Road, Charlotte

Harry L. Jones, Sr. Golf Cou Course – Tyvola Road, Charlotte

Dr. Charles L. Sifford Course – Barringer Drive, Charlotte

Sunset Hills – Radio Road, Charlotte

Boating

With water in every direction, as you might expect, boating is popular. Lake Norman—the largest area body of water—has the most commercial activity in terms of rentals and services. Numerous boat rental shops can provide you with a pontoon or a speedboat if you don't have your own. On Lake Norman there are eight public boat launches and 17 marinas that are home to boats of all types. There are many free launch spots, but even the ones that charge are around typically $2 – $3.

Anglers who want to dangle a hook quietly over the side of the boat can do it while the more serious fisherman will find a number of Bass and Striper tournaments on Norman, Wylie and Mountain Island. Fishing boat charters provide trips with guides who really know the lake's hotspots. Mecklenburg County even has a tackle loaner program if you want to try before you buy. A North Carolina fishing license is required.

Sailors will be most at home on Lake Norman. Yacht clubs here hold many weekend regattas. There is a sailing academy if you want to learn the finer points.

There are regattas for rowers, and you can take classes to be certified to have access for certain levels of boats. Dragon boating is getting very popular on Lake Norman. The community stages an annual Asian and Dragon Boat Festival each year in May.

Want to just relax and let someone else pilot your craft? There are Lake Norman dinner cruises on the Catawba Queen and the Lady of the Lake. Or, if you want to hold a private event on a boat, there's Yachta Yachta Yachta Charters and Luxury Yacht Cruises, among others.

Kayaks and canoes are popular on all the lakes but Mountain Island Lake is more conducive for a relaxing paddle. Mecklenburg Parks operate a kayak and canoeing instructional program, and rents canoes at Latta Plantation Park.

Charlotte is home to the US National Whitewater Center, the world's largest manmade river, which is complete with class three and four rapids for rafting or even kayaking for experienced paddlers.

Go Outside And Play

In Charlotte, we encourage you to play in the street at one of our many street fairs and festivals. Speed Street festival is mounted in uptown Charlotte during the week leading up to NASCAR's World

600 race. Another favorite in Charlotte is Festival in the Park, held every year in September since 1964 at Freedom Park.

We mentioned that we like food here, didn't we? Well, Taste of Charlotte happens annually the second week of June on the streets of uptown. Stroll down Tryon Street and enjoy a smorgasbord. Then there's the Soul of the South walking tour of uptown in October where you can sample culinary treats and even meet local chefs.

Enough about uptown. Despite its increasingly urban nature, Mecklenburg County still has lots of places where you can enjoy the great outdoors. There are 210 public county parks and facilities that cover more than 17,600 acres.

You'll find facilities ranging from smaller neighborhood type parks to the three heavily wooded nature centers--Latta Plantation, Reedy Creek and McDowell Park, and 17 more nature preserves. There are numerous trails in the larger parks for hiking, and you can camp at McDowell Park, which is on Lake Wylie as is nearby Copperhead Island.

There are 17 inclusive parks that feature wheelchair and walker accessible equipment, as well as swings with shoulder straps and high seat backs. Playgrounds at these parks contain equipment that offers visual, tactile and auditory stimulation.

The Park Department's Fitness & Wellness Division operate 20 recreation centers, too.

Five dog parks are spread across the county, giving local canines a chance to stretch their legs.

And, you don't just have to stay in Mecklenburg County, you know. In our survey of Charlotteans, a common theme mentioned was our proximity to the mountains and the beaches.

It's a quick trip of less than two hours to be in some of the most beautiful, rugged country you'll ever see. The Linville Gorge, often called the Grand Canyon of the East, is a favorite of veteran hikers. Still beautiful, but a little less strenuous to hike, is Black Balsam on the Blue Ridge Parkway outside of Asheville.

You can reach North Carolina's beaches near Wilmington in about three hours, and can travel to Charleston, SC in about the same amount of time.

When people say "wine country" North Carolina is not necessarily the first thing that comes to mind. Did you know that North Carolina now has more than 400 vineyards and 185 wineries spread from the mountains to the sea? Some produce wines from Muscadines, the native sweet grape of North Carolina. However, there are many wineries now producing good wines from Italian and French varietals. Our insider tip is to go to Junius Lindsay Vineyard outside of Lexington, NC to try wines made in the style of France's Rhone Valley.

What's The Attraction?

Charlotte has lots of attractions. One of our favorite spots is Discovery Place, the hands-on science museum in uptown. Great exhibits and education programs engage audiences of all ages as they learn about science, technology, engineering and math. Discovery Place also operates the Discovery Place KIDS Museum in Huntersville and the Charlotte Nature Museum adjacent to Freedom Park.

Source: Discovery Place

And the Carolina Raptor Center, in Latta Plantation Park, provides children as well as adults the opportunity to interact with large birds of prey.

Another kid favorite is Carowinds, a 398-acre theme park that straddles the North and South Carolina border just south of town. Boomerang Bay, a 20-acre water park located within Carowinds is a key summer attraction. Not to mention roller coasters.

Like to bowl? There's 10 Park Lanes in south Charlotte and there's StrikeCity, an upscale bowling and billiards facility uptown in the EPICENTRE complex.

Source: Carowinds

NASCAR fans can take behind the scenes tours of local race team facilities, or visit the NASCAR Hall of Fame uptown near the convention center. If you really have race fever, you might consider one of the racing experiences where you can ride around the track or even drive the car yourself.

One of the most visited attractions in Charlotte is the Billy Graham Library, which is a museum designed to be an on-going ministry that details the work of Charlotte-born evangelist Billy Graham.

Or, maybe a horse-drawn carriage ride through the streets of uptown is more to your liking. You can do that, too.

If you can't find something fun to do here in Charlotte, it's not our fault.

CHAPTER 8
KIDS TODAY

For families, childcare and education are important factors to consider when moving to a new area. Let's take a look at your choices in childcare, schools and other activities.

Infant and Toddler Care

Finding daycare in Charlotte is more a question of what type or level of care you prefer, since you have plenty of options. You can find nannies, au pairs, independently operated centers, as well as hospital and church-affiliated programs. Prices run the gamut and vary depending upon the age of your child, level of service, hours of operation and what part of the county you are in. In fact, the number of options can be overwhelming. For licensed childcare facilities in Mecklenburg County, the average cost for an infant is $200 per week.

There are a number of church run Mother's Morning Out programs that allow you to drop off your child for several hours while you run errands. If time is not of the essence, this often is a good first step, providing you an opportunity to connect with and get referrals from local moms at the church program.

How do you make an educated choice and assure that the center is safe?

Source: Carowinds

Luckily, there is help. The NC Division of Child Development and Early Education oversees all aspects of child care services in North Carolina, regulating child care facilities and overseeing the state's subsidized child care program. They offer financial assistance to help eligible families pay for child care. This agency ensures that standards are being maintained, and shuts down those that don't meet them. Additionally, they have a one to five star rating system to help you make a more informed decision.

When it comes to selection, Childcare Resources is there to help. This agency, which has been around since 1982, supports families by connecting them with information about services available in the community. Child Care Search is a service offered through Childcare Resources that provides a list of referrals to programs that meet your family's needs, including preferred type of care, location, operating hours, program costs, and licensing information. You may call Childcare Resources directly to discuss your needs, set up face-to-face appointments or utilize their web-based directory.

If you need to arrange childcare quickly, I recommend getting in touch with Childcare Resources as soon as possible since there are often waiting lists for the best centers, especially for those accepting infants.

As kids near school age, there are school system run programs available. Charlotte-Mecklenburg Schools (CMS) runs a pre-K program, Bright Beginnings, for at-risk four year olds. These centers, spread throughout the county, are run by CMS in conjunction with community based child care sites. Bright Beginnings serves as a model for similar programs around the country.

Children at higher levels of achievement and maturity can enter kindergarten early if they reach their fourth birthday by April 16.

Public and Private Schools

Charlotte has highly-rated public and private schools for your children.

CMS – the 18th largest school system in the nation—has recently won the Broad Prize for Urban Education for its improvement in elevating achievement levels. The system reports that it had the highest average scale scores in math among 21 urban districts in the 2015 National Assessment of Educational Progress. The district also ranked second in fourth-grade reading and third in eighth-grade reading.

The system operates a total of 164 schools that serve 145,112 students. It requires 10,798 teachers, who average 10.5 years of experience, to wrangle this many students. We have 91 elementary schools, 39 middle schools, 31 high schools and four alternative schools.

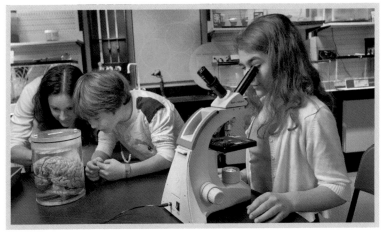

Source: Discovery Place

CMS runs 9 magnet school programs at 37 schools. Magnet program themes include center for leadership and global studies, international baccalaureate, learning immersion, science, technology engineering & math, military, Montessori, traditional visual & performing arts and world languages. North Carolina law requires all school systems to provide free transportation to any student who lives 1.5 miles or more from his assigned school. CMS has more than 955 buses that carry 123,000 students each school day.

As in anything else, you need to shop around to find the best schools for your child's needs. CMS assigns children to schools based upon their home address. So, this is where it becomes important to hire a realtor knowledgeable about the schools as you are home shopping. Or, you need to be lucky enough to win the lottery the school system runs to determine who gets into the magnet-school programs.

What are the best schools? Let's take a look at the top CMS public schools as rated by GreatSchools.org, which ranks schools from 1 to 10, 10 being the highest rated

TOP RANKED SCHOOLS

Elementary (all ranked 10)	Grades
Bain Elementary	K–5
Ballantyne Elementary	K–5
Beverly Woods	K–5
Collinswood Language Academy	K–8
Dilworth Elementary	K–5
Elon Park Elementary	K–5
Hawk Ridge Elementary	K–5
Irwin Academic Center	K–5
McKee Road Elementary	K–5
Metrolina Regional Scholars Academy	K–8
Olde Providence Elementary	K–5
Park Road Montessori	PK–6
Polo Ridge Elementary	K–5
Providence Spring Elementary	K–5
Selwyn Elementary	K–5
Sharon Elementary	K–5
Socrates Academy	K–8

TOP RANKED SCHOOLS

Middle schools (all ranked 10)	Grades
Community House Middle	6–8
Jay M. Robinson Middle School	6–8
Piedmont Open Middle School	6–8
South Charlotte Middle	6–8

High schools (all ranked 9)	Grades
Ardrey Kell High	9–12
Providence High	9–12

Source: GreatSchools.org

Rapid population growth in Charlotte has spurred on a building boom for CMS. Many new schools have been built in the past five years, and a $290 million 2013 bond package has outlined plans to build six new schools and to renovate or expand 11 other facilities.

According to www.cms.k12.nc.us, the CMS student population is 42% black, 32% white, 18% Hispanic, 5% Asian and 3% American Indian/multiracial. In 2012, 8,941 students graduated.

Graduation rates hit record highs of 85.1% last academic year, primarily by realizing significant gains among disadvantaged students. This rate was above the overall state rate of 82.5%.

The dropout rate has declined to 3.2%. CMS' annual budget is $1.3 billion, which equates to an expenditure of $8,473 per-pupil.

Some of Charlotte's private schools are top notch, but you'll pay for the quality. More than 26,000 students are enrolled in 85 private and charter schools, according to the Charlotte Chamber of Commerce.

Two of the best and oldest are Charlotte Country Day, Charlotte Latin. Tuition at these schools ranges from $15,000 – $22,000 annually. Country Day serves only 1660 students in pre-K through 12th grade. The curriculum is challenging and aims at getting students prepared for college. Charlotte Latin also has a good teacher to student ratio, since its enrollment is more than 1400. It, too, has a college preparatory curriculum.

Both schools are co-ed and nonsectarian. If you are looking for a racially diverse school, you'll need to look elsewhere. Both schools have student populations that are roughly 90% white.

Mountain Island Day School, Anami Montessori, and Dore Academy receive good grades for their results.

Other highly ranked private schools include the Catholic schools, such as St. Ann Catholic Elementary, St. Patrick Elementary, St. Gabriel Elementary, Our Lady of the Assumption Elementary, and Charlotte Catholic High. Charlotte Jewish Day School is also highly rated, as are Charlotte Christian School, Adventist Academy, Berean Junior Academy and United Faith Christian Academy.

Since there are more than 85 private schools in our area, this is not a definitive list. We have just tried to give you some options to consider. It is important to visit the schools you are considering to evaluate all of the variables.

One final note on education in Charlotte: a number of other organizations are involved in the process. The Charlotte-Mecklenburg Public Library operates an early literacy program, summer reading programs, and offers homework help after school. For teens the library has programs to ease the transition from high school to college or work

Parents' Night Out

When you move to a new city and don't have the luxury of family backup, it can be tough to find someone to keep the kids while you take a much-deserved night off. You can start with co-workers and neighbors for recommendations but often they don't want to give away the name of their favorite babysitter. Check with stay-at-home moms in your neighborhood who may want to earn some extra money.

Some neighborhood associations keep a directory of local kids who babysit. And a number of churches offer drop-off babysitting services or will know kids in the congregation who sit. Additionally, you can check with the local colleges to see if they have students who babysit as a way to earn a little spending money. When you do find a babysitter, the rate in Charlotte depends upon the age of the sitter and the number of kids you have. A typical fee would be in the $10 – 13 per hour range.

There are a number of Parents' Night Out programs run by the local YMCA, and a couple of commercial centers, such as Kids Klub and The Little Gym, that occasionally offer this service.

If you are still having trouble finding a sitter, you might try Childcare Resources, which keeps a directory of sitters, or *Charlotte Parent Magazine's* online directory.

Fun Activities for Young Ones

If your kids are bored, it won't be due to a lack of activities. The Charlotte Mecklenburg Parks operate programs for younger children at facilities around the county. You can register at E-Parks to see what programs are available. MeckTeens is a parks program aimed at 11 – 17-year-olds that provides social, physical and educational activities, life skill training and team building. Looking for a venue for the next birthday party? There's a good chance you'll find one you like at a local park.

Got swimmers? The park system operates the world-class natatorium Mecklenburg County Aquatic Center, Ray's Splash Planet, several neighborhood pools and numerous spraygrounds.

Source: Children's Theatre of Charlotte

Children's Theatre of Charlotte is one of the country's top theatre and education organizations for young people. It mounts 15 adult productions annually for young audiences. The theatre is home base for a fully professional touring company called The Taradiddle Players. And, the Children's Theatre puts on a range of enrichment classes and summer camps for your aspiring young actors.

Unless you tell your kids that ImaginOn is educational, they'll be having too much fun to figure it out. A collaborative project of Children's Theatre and the Public Library, ImaginOn's mission is to bring stories to life through extraordinary experiences that challenge, inspire and excite young minds.

Musical children might like the Charlotte Symphony's Lollipops Series where they explore music through hands-on activities. Or, if they are really musically precocious, let them audition for the Charlotte Symphony Youth Orchestras.

If the kids are into team sports, log on to www.charlotteyouthsports. com. This website connects you with area organizations that operate youth sports programs ranging from baseball to volley and martial arts to dance.

Small zoos where you can get close to the animals are all around the area. In Asheboro, NC, about an hour and a half from Charlotte, you'll find one of the finest natural habitat zoos in the world, the North Carolina Zoo. You'll see everything from elephants to gorillas and from hummingbirds to polar bears.

If you are a NASCAR fan, there's a chance your kids might have the racing bug. The Speedpark at Concord Mills is a go-karting facility where they can safely practice their driving skills.

Higher Education

Charlotte's higher education community is filled with excellent colleges, universities and technical schools, which offer a wide selection of post-high school opportunities. Both traditional and online options are available to you here.

Source: UNC Charlotte, Wade Bruton, photographer

University of North Carolina – Charlotte

On Charlotte's east side about eight miles from center city is UNCC, a 1,000-acre urban research institution that is home to 28,000 students, about 5,000 of whom are master's and doctoral candidates.

The University opened in 1946 to serve returning veterans. Today, it is the fourth largest of the 17 institutions within the University of North Carolina system.

Source: UNC Charlotte, Wade Bruton, photographer

UNCC features seven professional colleges which include the Belk College of Business, College of Arts + Architecture, College of Computing and Informatics, College of Education, College of Health and Human Services, College of Liberal Arts & Sciences, and William States Lee College of Engineering.

Roughly 1000 fulltime faculty members conduct 21 doctoral programs, 61 master's degree programs and 78 bachelor's degree programs. From accounting to theatre and from music to religious studies, UNCC offers something for everyone. The most popular current majors at UNCC are business, management, marketing, engineering, health professions, social sciences and education.

Four years ago, UNCC opened its Center City campus in uptown Charlotte, where it conducts a number of master's level classes.

UNCC is accredited to award baccalaureate, master's and doctorate degrees from the Commission of Colleges of the Southern Association of Colleges and Schools. The university's master of business administration program has been ranked in the top 50 part-time degree programs by *U.S. News & World Report.*

The Metropolitan Studies Group comprises all of the university's community based research organizations. Its highly regarded Urban Institute has for more than 40 years sought solutions to the social, economic and environmental challenges facing local communities.

Outside of class this campus bustles with activity year-round. Students enjoy top quality music, dance and theatrical performances. Art galleries on campus mount exhibitions regularly. The university hosts internationally renowned speakers who address topics of local and national interest.

Facilities include a fitness center, aerobics studio, indoor climbing wall, swimming pool and recreational courts that are free of charge to students. A variety of sports clubs, intramurals and fitness program also are available.

And, then there are the collegiate level sports. The Charlotte 49ers athletics teams are members of Conference USA and compete on the NCAA Division I level. UNCC funds 17 sports teams, including baseball, men's and women's basketball, men's and women's cross country, golf, men's and women's soccer, softball, men's and women's tennis, men's and women's indoor and outdoor track and field, and volleyball. In the fall of 2013, the 49ers started the inaugural season of its football program.

Source: UNC Charlotte, Wade Bruton, photographer

Its biggest sports success has come on the hardwood. The 49ers reached the NCAA Final Four basketball tournament in 1977 and have regularly reached the playoffs since then. UNCC has sent eight players on to the NBA.

Queens University

I have a soft spot for this local University because my wife and I were wed in Queens' Belk Chapel. Founded by the Presbyterian Church in 1857 as the Charlotte Female Institute, Queens University is sited on a beautiful, wooded campus in the historic Myers Park neighborhood only two miles from center city. It is known for its lovely Georgian brick buildings and park-like setting. The university's Presbyterian School of Nursing is located uptown on Fifth Street. The school admitted its first male students after World War II.

The Commission on Colleges of the Southern Association of Colleges and Schools accredited Queens to award bachelor's and master's degrees. Queens offers 39 majors, 74 minors and 11 graduate degree programs through its College of Arts & Sciences, McColl School of Business, Knight School of Communication, Cato School of Education, Blair College of Health and School of Graduate and Continuing Studies. Graduate programs offered include master's degrees in education, teaching, nursing,

Source: Queens University

communications, creative writing, organizational development, music theory and interior design. Only 2,250 students are enrolled currently, 71% of whom are on-campus residents. They are served by 122 full-time faculty members, which give the university an enviable 12:1 student to faculty ratio. The average class size is 14 students.

Specialized campus centers include Internships and Career Center, the Center for International Education, the Center for Ethics and Religion, the Center for Entrepreneurial Leadership, the Center for Active Citizenship and the Center for the Advancement of Faculty Excellence.

U.S. News & World Report ranked Queens #20 on its 2016 list of top regional universities in the south. Other awards include *The Chronicle of Higher Education's* Best College To Work For, and Best Place in Charlotte to Work by the *Charlotte Business Journal.*

Education is important here but Queens focuses on the developing well-rounded individual by promoting global understanding and ethical living as well as intellectual curiosity.

Clubs ranging from art and dance to gospel choir and martial arts are available to all students. Queens lets students choose five national sororities and two national fraternities.

Tradition is important on the Queens campus. Each year the Boar's Head Banquet and Yule Log Ceremony warms up the Christmas season. Casino Night, a formal event full of dancing, music and casino tables, is another favorite.

Keeping students healthy and fit is an important factor for Queens. To that end, they have a student health and wellness center and are building the new Levine Center for Wellness and Recreation.

A Division II school, Queens offers a total of 20 men's and women's sports. The Royals have had successes recently in men's basketball, cross country, tennis and both men's and women's soccer.

Johnson & Wales – Charlotte

One thing is certain, since Johnson & Wales University (JWU) opened its uptown Charlotte campus in 2003, our restaurants have improved immeasurably. On this highly urban campus, 2,500 students from 46 states and 23 countries learn their trade in the College of Culinary Arts, the Hospitality College, and the College of Business.

Source: Applewood Gallery and Imaging – Johnson & Wales

JWU offers degreed programs in baking & pastry, business, culinary arts, fashion merchandising, hotel and lodging management, management, marketing, restaurant, food & beverage management, and sports, entertainment & event management.

The New England Association of Schools & Colleges has accredited JWU through its Commission on Institutions of Higher Education. Additionally, the UNC Board of Governors has licensed the university to conduct degree activity in North Carolina.

The glass and stone tower at the campus Trade Street entrance is impressive, and you can peek in street-level windows to catch a glimpse of the chocolate and sugar-pulling labs.

As you might expect of a culinary school, many of the student organizations have a definite bent toward food. There's the Baking & Pastry Club, Molecular Gastronomy Club, Future Business Leaders of America, and the Fashion Society.

The Charlotte campus has recently opened a new 30,000-square-foot student center that features a fitness center and a 600 seat gymnasium.

JWU is a member of the United States Collegiate Athletic Association and the Charlotte campus fields intercollegiate teams in women's volleyball and men's basketball. The school also sponsors competitive club teams in ice hockey, cheerleading, women's basketball, men's volleyball and men's and women's soccer.

Davidson College

You should be noticing a theme among Charlotte's colleges and universities: the Presbyterian Church was instrumental in starting many of them, including Davidson College, 20 minutes north of uptown Charlotte. The liberal arts college was established in 1837, and named for William Lee Davidson, a Revolutionary War hero.

The original 665-acre forested campus is home to about 1950 male and female students. Today, there is also a 110-acre lake campus, which is a popular recreation spot for students, faculty and staff. The club sailing and crew teams call this campus home.

Davidson College focuses on the liberal arts, offering roughly 26 majors, 17 minors plus interdisciplinary studies, ranging from anthropology to Greek and from history to writing. Many Davidson students opt to take pre-professional programs such as pre-law, pre-medicine, pre-military and pre-ministry. The school is accredited in awarding baccalaureate degrees by the Southern Association of Colleges and Schools Commission on Colleges. About 71% of Davidson's students will take advantage of the college's excellent study abroad program, which includes the renowned Dean Rusk International Studies Program. The college boasts of a 10:1 student to faculty ratio.

U.S. News & World Report ranks Davidson College #9 among US liberal arts colleges. It is alma mater to 23 Rhodes Scholars and was the first liberal arts college to eliminate loans in financial aid packages.

Study of the arts is an important part of Davidson's liberal arts education. The campus has several venues for the arts, including Duke Family Performance Hall, Sloan Music Center, and Cunningham Theatre Center. Additionally, Davidson College Presbyterian Church has facilities often used for performances.

In addition to arts and culture, students have opportunities to participate in other shared interests through more than 200 organizations. Academics, recreational sports, politics, service organizations, as well as fraternities and sororities help develop well-rounded students.

Collegiate sports have long been important at Davidson, which competes in 11 men's sports and 10 women's sports, primarily in the Division 1 Southern Conference. It joined the Atlantic 10 Conference in 2014. The Wildcats have participated in NCAA sports since 1920 and during that time have made appearances in men's basketball, men's soccer and women's volleyball NCAA championships, as well as winning the Women's Tennis National title.

Johnson C. Smith University

Once on this wooded campus that is steeped in history, you can barely tell that you are in the shadows of uptown's skyscrapers.

In 1867, this historically black college was founded by—you guessed it—Presbyterians, who saw a need for higher education of recently freed slaves. The college was initially called The Freedmen's College of North Carolina. Its name was changed to Biddle University the year of its founding to recognize a generous contribution from Mary D. Biddle.

Biddle played in—and won—the first ever black college football game in 1892 against Livingstone College, which is still a rival today. It became in 1919 the first black college in the South to offer professional courses in education. In 1921, the late Jane Berry Smith provided a handsome endowment and the school was renamed to Johnson C. Smith University (JCSU), in memory of her late husband. The Romanesque-style Biddle Memorial Hall, which sits on the highest point in Charlotte, was listed on the National Register of Historic Places in 1975.

JCSU has 1,402 students, who have 22 fields of study from which to choose in three colleges: the College of Arts and Letters, the College of STEM, and the College of Professional Studies. An 11:1 student to faculty ratio makes this an attractive educational option to both in-state and out-of-state students. The university is accredited by the Southern Association of Colleges and Schools and National Council for the Accreditation of Teacher Education.

U.S. News & World Report ranks JCSU 16th among all historically black colleges and universities. It is a member of the Clinton Global Initiative, and was named to the President's Higher Education Community Service Honor Roll in 2010, 2011, 2012, 2013, and 2014.

More than 60 organizations vie for JCSU students' attention. There's a large Greek community, as well as many arts and culture-related groups.

Six men's collegiate sports and seven women's collegiate sports are offered through the athletic department. JCSU is a member of the NCAA – Division II, and the Central Intercollegiate Athletic Association.

Source: CPCC

Adult Education

There are a host of other business, professional and technical schools, colleges and universities in Charlotte, including the NASCAR Technical Institute, which provides hands-on training with the world's top auto and diesel brands.

No discussion of continuing education would be complete without mentioning Central Piedmont Community College, or CPSS as we all call it.

CPCC offers two-year programs, many transferable to four-year schools, as well as corporate learning, workplace learning and personal enrichment courses through its network of six campuses throughout the county. It is accredited by the Southern Association of Colleges and Schools to award associate degrees, diplomas and certificates.

Accounting, advertising and graphic design, criminal justice, culinary arts, dental hygiene, health information, horticulture and transfer programs in the arts, fine arts and science are just a few of the opportunities student may pursue here. CPCC began modestly with just 1600 students and a dozen degree programs to more than 258 degree, diploma, and certificate programs. When you add on-site corporate training, ESL, GED and non-college courses, CPSS serves more than 70,000 people each year.

Source: CPCC

The school is emerging as a cultural resource, as it offers not only opportunities to study the arts, but to see performances and exhibits. The college has on-campus performances mounted by CPCC Theatre, Summer Theatre, Opera Theatre, as well as many dance and music performances.

CHAPTER 9
FITTING IN

In the survey we did for the book, we asked people to rate various attributes. "Friendliness of the people" received the third highest ranking behind "neighborhood in which you live" and "weather." We agree that the people are one of the best things about Charlotte.

But you sometimes hear naysayers complaining that Charlotte is cliquish. Those are the people who lack a positive, can-do attitude, or who see Charlotte only as a career stepping stone and who have no desire to be or stay here. Fitting in here means getting involved.

One of the first things your new neighbors or office cohorts may ask you when you move here is if you have found a church yet. This bothers some people, but it is just our way of trying to help you fit in. Charlotte has plenty of church options for you, and can be a very good way for you to ease your transition into your new hometown. Charlotte's faith-based community provides excellent volunteer opportunities that can help you learn more about the area and the people.

The Charlotte Rescue Mission, a Christian Recovery program, helps people caught in poverty and addictions. It hosts several volunteer orientations each month. The Salvation Army of Greater Charlotte is also always welcoming volunteers. Or, contact Mecklenburg Ministries, an interfaith, interracial organization that brings congregations together to address community issues.

Crisis Assistance Ministries was begun in the midst of the recession in the 1970s, when faith-based benevolence funds, food pantries and clothing closets were overwhelmed by demand. Its mission is to assist the working poor who are in financial crisis. Volunteers perform about 1/3 of the work at Crisis Assistance, and they could use your help.

There are secular volunteer opportunities as well. One of our favorites is Hands-On Charlotte, a nonprofit volunteer service organization that promotes volunteerism and direct community service to meet Charlotte's most critical needs. Hands-On currently has opportunities for volunteers with building skills, those who can tutor in reading and basic math, be a bi-lingual story time assistant, even a high school mentor.

Making a Difference in Charlotte

By Michael Marsicano

When I arrived in Charlotte from Durham in 1989 to lead our Arts & Science Council (ASC), I was struck by the collective generosity of my new city. Our community's per capita donations to the ASC's annual giving campaign grew to number one among the nation's United Art Fund drives. The citizens of Charlotte valued our arts and cultural organizations and they joined forces—ten, twenty, fifty dollars at a time—to ensure the sustainability of these beloved institutions.

Back then, Charlotte was led by a few revered business leaders who collaboratively shaped our city's future. There was a real sense of public-private partnership and a commitment to Charlotte's growth and prosperity. In recent years, we have seen a dramatic shift in leadership. We rely more on generous, committed and diverse citizens who have the drive and determination to move our city forward. And where there is a need for a larger civic leader and community catalyst, Foundation For The Carolinas works diligently to fill that role.

Since 1999, I have had the privilege of leading Foundation For The Carolinas, the Charlotte region's home for philanthropy and civic engagement. As a community foundation we serve as a catalyst for charitable good, connecting people to philanthropic opportunities and needs across our region.

By convening diverse groups of citizens of widely varying professions, cultural backgrounds, financial status and political leanings, we have joined forces to address our region's most critical issues and biggest opportunities. For example, when the economic crisis hit this financial epicenter hard in 2007, our citizens gave millions of dollars to help feed, clothe and shelter our neighbors in crisis.

When preserving green space became a pressing need, a group of citizens launched plans for the Carolina Thread Trail, a network of greenways that will eventually weave together 15 counties throughout our region across more than 1,400 miles.

And when an area school's graduation rates needed a boost, philanthropists and civic leaders worked with the school system and the community to create Project L.I.F.T., a major educational initiative that is making a profound difference in our public schools and in the lives of our most vulnerable students.

In view of the transformative impact on the community, these innovative initiatives attracted large-scale donations by individual families. Over time we have combined large corporate giving with grassroots giving and, more recently, significant gifts from generous families, to create real and lasting impact in Charlotte. When committed groups of citizens rally to lift our community, we call that civic leadership. It is these civic-minded neighbors and friends that make Charlotte a great place to live.

One of the best ways you can join the fabric of our community is it to volunteer your time, talent or treasure. Making a difference in Charlotte doesn't require great amounts of money; only a passion and a desire to shape the future of this vibrant community.

Michael Marsicano is President and Chief Executive Officer of Foundation For The Carolinas. Managing assets, owned and represented, of approximately $1.61 billion, the Foundation holds over 1900 charitable funds. In the sixteen years Dr. Marsicano has been at the helm of FFTC, contributions to the Foundation have totaled more than $1.61 billion and grant awards more than $1 billion.

Join The Club

Charlotte has a wealth of alumni groups, book clubs, civic or professional organizations and interest groups. If you want to network with like-minded individuals, you can do it here.

There's the Black Political Caucus, Charlotte Dance Gypsies, Davidson Community Players, the Guild of Charlotte Artists, Loch Norman Pipe Band, NC Association of CPAs, American Marketing Association, a slew of Rotary and Civitan groups, as well as the Italian Club, Charlotte Rugby Club, Queen City Model A Club and Daughters of the American Revolution. That is just the tip of the iceberg.

Sports teams also bring people together in Charlotte. Since almost every Charlottean but me is from somewhere else, they probably support a football team other than the Carolina Panthers. There's an online list of NFL Football Meetups held in Charlotte to help you find your team. Many fans have taken over certain venues. Here's where fans watch their games:

- Buffalo Bills – Tavern on the Tracks

- Cleveland Browns – Kennedy's Premium Bar & Grill

- Philadelphia Eagles – Steamer's Sports Pub

- Pittsburgh Steelers – Fitzgerald's Irish Pub

Your homeowner's association also can be a good resource for you. Many of the larger, new neighborhoods have events, as well as websites where you can learn what's happening in your community. These are a good place to meet your neighbors.

The Media

Local TV Stations

- WBTV – Channel 3 (CBS)

- WSOC – Channel 9 (ABC)

- WHKY – Channel 14 (Ind.)

- WCCB – Channel 18 (CW)

- WCNC – Channel 36 (NBC)

- WTVI – Channel 42 (PBS)

- WJZY – Channel 46 (Fox)

- WUNG – Channel 58 (PBS)

- WAXN – Channel 64 (Ind.)

Local Radio Stations – FM

- WDAV – 89.9 (Classical, NPR)

- WFAE – 90.7 (News/Talk, NPR)

- WQNC – 92.7(Hip Hop)

- WNKS – 95.1 (Top 40)

- WKKT – 96.9 (Country)

- WPEG – 97.9 (Mainstream Urban)

- WRFX – 99.7 (Classic Rock)
- WBAC – 101.9 (Urban Adult Contemporary)
- WSOC-FM – 103.7 (Country)
- WKQC – 104.7 (Adult Contemporary)
- WOLS – 106.1 (Spanish)
- WEND – 106.5 (Modern Rock)
- WLNK – 107.9 (1990's to Now Rock)

Local Radio Stations – AM

- WFNZ – 610 AM (Sports)
- WYFQ – 930 AM (Religious)
- WBT – 1110 AM (News/Talk)
- WHVN – 1240 AM (Religious)
- WGSP – 1310 AM (Spanish)
- WGFY – 1480 AM (Religious)
- WOGR – 1540 (Religious)
- WBCN – 1660 (Talk)

Local Print Media

The Charlotte Observer (daily newspaper)

Charlotte Business Journal (weekly business newspaper)

The Charlotte Jewish News (monthly magazine)

The Charlotte Post (weekly newspaper)

Charlotte Magazine (monthly magazine)

Business North Carolina (monthly magazine)

Creative Loafing (weekly newspaper)

Charlotte Parent (monthly magazine)

Ballantyne Magazine (monthly magazine)

Lake Norman Magazine (monthly magazine)

SouthPark Magazine (monthly magazine)

Greater Charlotte Biz (monthly magazine)

Mecklenburg Times (weekly newspaper)

Lake Norman Citizen (weekly newspaper)

The Herald Weekly (weekly newspaper)

South Charlotte Weekly (weekly newspaper)

CHAPTER 10

MAKING THE MOVE

Unlike beach destinations, Charlotte is a year-round town. So, there is no need to consider when the Canadians are heading back north. And since we have great weather year-round, that's not much of an issue either.

We may have some snowy days in January, February and March, but we rarely get enough accumulation to hamper your move.

So, you have several options: move yourself, hire a mover, or go all out and hire a personal relocation consultant to handle all the details.

No matter which you choose, there are a few items you'll need to consider. First, think about what you will need in Charlotte. If you are moving from the northeast, you won't need the snow shovel and some of the heavy winter clothing can probably go, too. In Charlotte, few houses have basements, so that additional storage space won't be available to you. You may want to take this opportunity to downsize your collection of antique tractors. Seriously, this can be a prime opportunity to get rid of unwanted items either by donating to charity or holding a garage sale.

You may even want to sell your home furnished and once in North Carolina take advantage of the great pricing we have on furniture.

Do you have a Plan B? Sometimes things happen between selling a house in one location and buying or renting somewhere else. If your move-in date shifts because of a rescheduled mortgage closing, where will you stay in Charlotte until your home is ready? There are a number of extended stay options, as well as numerous hotels, some probably near your new home. It's a good idea to have a backup plan and have contact information for them in advance.

If you are hiring a mover, there are some pricing variables to consider. The first is what day to move. It costs more to move on Friday, Saturday or Sunday than on a weekday. Also, moving at the end of the month costs more because leases are expiring and there is more demand. Moving with school age children presents some unique complications as well. A summer move gives your kids a chance to acclimate a bit before school starts.

So, if you have some flexibility, choose a weekday near the middle of a summer month. Remember, too, that a mover typically provides a window of time to arrive, but they are at the mercy of the previous customer. Try to get an early morning time window, if possible.

Finally, movers offer levels of service. If you want to pack and unpack your own belongings, this can save you some money. Many movers will both pack and unpack for you. If you choose this option, have a plan as to where you want your items to go in your new home. This speeds up the move.

OK, you have decided to do the move yourself, so Uncle Billy and your cousins have come to help. They get you all loaded up but they don't come with you to Charlotte. There are a number of local loading and unloading services you may call for assistance. Elite Moving Labor and Moving Help are two that can help.

If you find that you need to store some items after your move, plenty of self-storage units are available throughout the county, including:

American Storage of Charlotte

DMI Storage

Penny Pinchers Storage

Public Storage of Charlotte

Any move is stressful, a cross country move even more so. That's where you might want the assistance of a full service moving concierge. They will get estimates and retain a mover for you, meet with the mover to plan and execute the move out and the move in.

CHAPTER 11

OUR DIVERSIFIED ECONOMY

Since 2000, the county's population has increased from 695,454 to 1,012,539 in 2014. Why?

As they have for decades, people come to Charlotte because they know they can find a well-paying job here. This is substantiated by Mecklenburg County's solid 2013 household income figures. Twenty-six percent of households have incomes in the $25,000 – $49,999 range, 18% range from $50,000 – $74,999, and 34% have incomes of $75,000 and over.

WHY PEOPLE MOVE TO CHARLOTTE

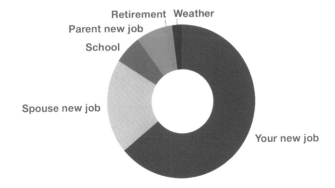

In the past, Charlotte was widely known for being a textile center and then a banking hub. That is true but overlooks the fact that we have a highly diversified economy that today runs the gamut from retail to manufacturing and finance to high tech.

Charlotte's leaders have worked hard to find the right balance. Figures from the Division of Employment Security show that in Mecklenburg County employment breaks down this way: 52,241 work in finance and insurance, 59,380 are in retail trade, 33,771 are in wholesale trade, 34,366 work in manufacturing and 19,727 are in information.

The presence of Fortune 500 operations in a community speak to its economic state. A total of 291 Fortune 500 companies are represented in Charlotte, eight of which are headquartered in our region. According to the Charlotte Chamber, there are 4,220 companies in Mecklenburg County with sales exceeding $1 million, 42 of which have sales that surpass the $1 billion mark. Nearly 1,000 of these are headquartered here.

Interestingly, Mecklenburg County has almost 1000 manufacturing firms operating here, more than any other county in the Carolinas. Once upon a time, cotton was our chief manufactured product. Not anymore. We now make medical and dental products, plastics, optical technology and even defense-related products.

Charlotte Can-Do!

By Bob Morgan

Charlotte is the 17th largest city in the United States. Charlotte Douglas International Airport has the 6th most flights nationwide. We like to brag about our ability to play above our weight. We are ambitious for our city. We want others to know that.

An orientation toward progressive growth is in our civic DNA. The original settlers competed for attention by naming their new town after the wife of King George III and their new county, Mecklenburg, after the region in Germany from whence she came.

When that same king threatened the liberties and economic freedoms of the colonies, our forefathers were among the first to rebel. Captain James Jack left Charlotte on May 20, 1775, headed to Philadelphia, to proclaim to the world the news of the Mecklenburg Declaration of Independence, more than a year before the more famous declaration of July 4, 1776. (Those who believe this history are true Charlotteans. Those who don't we call Charlatans!)

In the 1800s, Charlotte welcomed the railroads. In the 1900s, it was the interstates and then the airport. We want to be connected to the world, and we want the world to be connected to us. We are a forward-looking community.

Sixty eight percent of Charlotte's adult residents were born outside of the state of North Carolina. More come from the Northeast and Midwest than anywhere else. Many are "half backs," a term that describes Floridians who after the second or third hurricane don't want to go all the way back to Cleveland or Detroit.

Young people graduating from colleges and universities up and down the East Coast are moving here in large numbers. African-American professional families, as part of a reverse migration back to the Sun Belt, are most destined for Atlanta, Dallas and Charlotte, in that order, according to Black Enterprise magazine. The Latin American population has grown by more than 150 percent since 2000. We are not considered a "global city" by academic standards, but our region is home to almost 1,000 foreign-owned companies, and the foreign-born population is growing faster here than in most other cities.

In the new century, Charlotte is among the fastest-growing regions in the United States. People and companies are attracted to the jobs provided by a diverse range of employers in the banking, healthcare, energy, manufacturing, life sciences, motorsports, logistics, tourism and professional services industries.

People and companies are also attracted by the presence of professional sports; world-class cultural offerings; high-quality, cost competitive health care; a diverse and affordable housing stock; 39 institutions of higher learning; an incredibly vibrant, clean, safe and well organized center city; moderate weather; NASCAR; and the U.S. National Whitewater Center on the Catawba River.

We continue to tell the world about Charlotte. Hosting the Democratic National Convention in 2012 provided an unprecedented opportunity to do just that, with more than 15,000 visitors, including some 300 from 150 different countries around the world. They saw our city and they enjoyed our hospitality. Super Bowls and the Olympics are now in our vision for the future.

We appreciate this opportunity to tell others about Charlotte. When you finish this book, you can do the same!

Like most Charlotteans, Bob Morgan is a transplant. He was born in Rome, NY and moved to Charlotte with his family in 1971. Bob graduated from Charlotte's Independence High School and the University of North Carolina—Chapel Hill. Bob was named president and CEO of the Charlotte Chamber of Commerce in 2005.

Important Employers

Charlotte ranks in the top 20 among cities with Fortune 500 corporate headquarters. There are six that call Mecklenburg County home, plus two more headquartered in adjacent counties.

Bank of America—with $101.7 billion in revenues, is ranked 21 on the Fortune 500 list. The bank is also one of our largest employers with 15,000 workers in Mecklenburg County.

Lowe's is next at #56. The home improvement retailer, which is headquartered in Iredell County, has $53.4 billion in annual revenues and has 8,500 local employees.

At #123 on the Fortune list is Duke Energy, America's largest electric power holding company. Headquartered in Charlotte, it has $24.6 billion in revenues and employs 7,700 workers.

Behind Duke Energy at #150 is Nucor, an integrated steel company that has $19.1 billion in annual revenues. Nucor is the largest steel producer in the US, and most of its employees are at plants spread throughout the country.

Family Dollar Stores, with $10.4 billion in revenues, ranks at #271 on the Fortune list. This chain of variety stores is headquartered in Matthews, NC, and most of Family Dollar's employees are in their 7,100 stores located in 45 states.

Sonic Automotive, #309 on the list with $8.8 billion in revenues, is one of America's largest retailers of automobiles. It operates more than 100 auto dealerships in 14 states and 25 major metropolitan markets.

Sealed Air, the bubble wrap folks, have just relocated their HQ to Charlotte. They are #366 on the Fortune 500 with $7.8 billion in revenues.

Domtar, #469 on the Fortune 500 list with $5.4 billion in revenue, is the largest integrated manufacturer of uncoated paper in North America and the second largest in the world. It is headquartered in Fort Mill, SC.

It's Your Business

But it's not all about the big boys. Charlotte plays well with smaller firms. In fact, of the nearly 28,000 companies with Charlotte operations, roughly 26,000 of them employ fewer than 50 workers. Additionally, there are 4,100 small minority-owned businesses in Charlotte.

Entrepreneur Magazine called Charlotte one of its best cities for small business thanks to a steady migration of young workers, a business friendly banking community and a high-quality labor force with a low-cost labor environment. CNNMoney.com ranked Charlotte #8 on its list of 100 best places to live and launch a business. Forbes named it #14 on its list of Best Places for Business and Careers.

There are plenty of resources here to help you if you own or plan to start a business. Begin with the Charlotte Chamber of Commerce. It offers opportunities for you to network with the large and the small established businesses in our town. It also runs the Power Up Challenge, an award program that identifies promising startups and small businesses. Don't forget to check out the Chamber's Small Business Toolkit.

Central Piedmont Community College runs the Institute for Entrepreneurship, and UNC Charlotte offers an entrepreneurship certificate program. Also, Charlotte Business Resources connects you with the information you need to start a business here.

Employment Market

Charlotte's largest public employers are the Charlotte-Mecklenburg Schools, the City of Charlotte and North Carolina State Government. Our largest private employers include Carolinas Healthcare System, Wells Fargo, and the Bank of America.

Here are the top 25 employers in our region:

CHARLOTTE REGION'S LARGEST EMPLOYERS: 2015

Rank	Company	Employment
1.	Carolinas Healthcare	35,000
2.	Wells Fargo	22,000
3.	Charlotte-Mecklenburg Schools	18,143
4.	Wal-Mart Stores	16,100
5.	Bank of America	15,000
6.	Lowe's Corporation	12,960
7.	Novant Health	11,000
8.	American Airlines	10,600
9.	Harris Teeter Supermarkets	8,239
10.	Duke Energy	7,800
11.	North Carolina State Government	7,684
12.	Delhaize America Inc.	6,900
13.	City of Charlotte	6,000
14.	U.S. Government	5,360
15.	Daimler Trucks North America LLC	5,200
16.	Compass Group North America	4,860
17.	Mecklenburg County	4,520
18.	Union County Public Schools	4,456
19.	U.S. Postal Service	4,000
20.	Caromont Health	3,980
21.	Gaston County Schools	3,824
22.	Cabarrus County Schools	3,803
23.	AT&T North Carolina	3,290
24.	Time Warner Cable, Inc.	3,100
25.	University of North Carolina at Charlotte	3,100

Source: Charlotte Chamber of Commerce

Charlotte's unemployment rate spiked to 12.5% during the height of the recent recession but has moved steadily downward, dropping to 3.8% in the 3rd quarter of 2017. Salaries are bouncing back, too. As of late 2017, the average salary is $77.271, according to SalaryList. com. The median salary in Charlotte is $70,965. North Carolina's minimum wage is synced to the federal minimum wage, which as of this writing is $7.25 per hour.

20 MOST POPULAR JOBS

Rank	Title	Total Employees	Mean Salary
1	Office and Administrative Support Occupations	178480	$36,750
2	Sales and Related Occupations	133910	$45,870
3	Food Preparation and Serving Related Occupations	103640	$21,840
4	Transportation and Material Moving Occupations	92310	$34,700
5	Production Occupations	83860	$36,360
6	Business and Financial Operations Occupations	79940	$76,090
7	Healthcare Practitioners and Technical Occupations	60800	$80,410
8	Management Occupations	60520	$ 129,950
9	Education, Training, and Library Occupations	56780	$44,170
10	Installation, Maintenance, and Repair Occupations	48080	$46,810
11	Construction and Extraction Occupations	44390	$39,500
12	Computer and Mathematical Occupations	43500	$87,210
13	Retail Salespersons	39320	$26,370
14	Combined Food Preparation and Serving Workers, Including Fast Food	36620	$18,440
15	Building and Grounds Cleaning and Maintenance Occupations	30610	$25,480
16	Healthcare Support Occupations	29970	$27,200
17	Customer Service Representatives	29770	$36,450
18	Personal Care and Service Occupations	29500	$24,970
19	Protective Service Occupations	27410	$37,700
20	Cashiers	26900	$19,840

Other Economic Indicators

Real estate activity is an indicator of economic health, and Charlotte's activity is moving back into the black. Despite a recent uptick in mortgage rates, we're seeing increased construction in the single family home market here, as well as increasing new home sales.

The inventory of homes on the market declined 19.4% in December 2017 compared to December 2016, according to the Carolina Regional Realtors Association, while the average sales price increased 8.4% to$281,567.

A number of new apartment communities have been announced in the last several years, as well, an indicator that commercial construction is rebounding, too. And several major hotels have recently completed renovations, indicating that our tourism business is strengthening. Those are all good signs that we're on the mend.

CONCLUSION

Charlotteans don't like to brag. Oh, who am I kidding? Of course, we do. We have everything any optimistic, can-do type of person could want in a city

Our great weather beckons you to spend time outside in every season. Beautiful neighborhoods can be found in every corner of our county, ensuring you can find just what you want, where you want it. Jobs are readily available thanks to our strong, diversified economy, and living here is highly affordable.

Finally, friendly people are awaiting to welcome you to your new home. Come visit us and you'll see that Charlotte is your kind of place.

Don't forget to sign up at our blog, www.movingtocharlotteguide.com, and be sure to let us know when you get unpacked here in Charlotte.

ONLINE RESOURCES

Government Services

City of Charlotte – Mecklenburg County Government
www.charmeck.org
Dial 311 and an operator will direct your call to the appropriate City
or County department.

NC Driver's License
www.ncdot.gov/dmv/contact
919-715-7000
Fishing License
www.ncwildlife.org/default.aspx
919-707-0010

Boat Registration
www.ncwildlife.org/Boating/RegistrationTitling.aspx
800-628-3773

Marriage License
www.meckrod.manatron.com
Dial 311 and an operator will direct your call to the appropriate City
or County department.

Social Security
www.socialsecurity.gov/careers/locations.html
800-772-1213

Tax Collector
www.charmeck.org/mecklenburg/county/taxes/Pages/default.
aspx?src=hh
Dial 311 and an operator will direct your call to the appropriate City
or County department.

Vehicle Registration
www.ncdot.gov/dmv/vehicle
919-715-7000

Voter Registration
www.charmeck.org/mecklenburg/county/BOE/voter/Pages/
VoterRegistrationApplication.aspx
Dial 311 and an operator will direct your call to the appropriate City
or County department.

Utilities and Garbage Collection

Duke Energy
www.duke-energy.com/North-Carolina.asp
888-777-9898

Piedmont Natural Gas
www.piedmontng.com/about/aboutpng/customerservice/
startserviceresidential.aspx
800-752-7504

Charlotte-Mecklenburg Utilities
www.charmeck.org/city/charlotte/Utilities/Pages/Home.aspx
Dial 311 and an operator will direct your call to the appropriate City
or County department.

Charlotte Garbage Collection
www.charmeck.org/services/category/pages/garbageandrecycling.aspx
Dial 311 and an operator will direct your call to the appropriate City
or County department.

Cable Services

Time Warner Cable
www.timewarnercableoffers.com/north-carolina/
mecklenburg/?cb%5Bxp%5D=lptest
1-855-294-5233

MI-Connection (available in North Mecklenburg)
www.mi-connection.com
704-660-2840

Bus Service

Charlotte Area Transit System
www.charmeck.org/city/charlotte/cats/bus/routes/pages/default.aspx
Dial 311 and an operator will direct your call to the appropriate City
or County department.

Greyhound
www.greyhound.com/en/locations/locations.aspx?state=NC
704-375-3332

Business Assistance

Charlotte Chamber of Commerce
www.charlottechamber.com
704-378-1300

Charlotte-Mecklenburg Business Licenses
www.charmeck.org/mecklenburg/county/TaxCollections/
BusinessTaxes/Pages/PrivilegeLicense.aspx
Dial 311 and an operator will direct your call to the appropriate City
or County department.

SCORE
www.charlottescore.org/directions.php
704-344-6576

Hospitals

Carolinas Medical Center
www.carolinashealthcare.org/
704-355-2000

Carolinas Medical Center – Mercy
www.carolinashealthcare.org/default.cfm?id=2487&fr=true
704-379-5000

Carolinas Medical Center – University
www.carolinashealthcare.org/default.cfm?id=827&fr=true
704-548-6000

Novant Health Presbyterian Medical Center
www.presbyterian.org/
704-384-4000

Novant Health Huntersville Medical Center
www.presbyterianhospitalhuntersville.org/
704-316-4000

Novant Health Matthews Medical Center
www.presbyterianhospitalmatthews.org/
704-384-6500

Novant Health Charlotte Orthopedic Hospital
www.presbyterianorthopaedichospital.org/
704-316-2000

Police Non-Emergency

Charlotte-Mecklenburg Police Department
www.charmeck.org/city/charlotte/CMPD/Pages/default.aspx
704-336-7600

Education

Charlotte Mecklenburg Schools
www.cms.k12.nc.us/
704-343-5139

Newcomer Information

Charlotte Chamber
www.charlottechamber.com/main/newcomers/
704-378-1300

Charlotte, NC Travel & Tourism
www.charlottesgotalot.com/
704-331-2700

Charlotte Arts & Science Culture Guide
www.charlottecultureguide.com/
704-333-2272

ACKNOWLEDGEMENTS

No book is the work of any one person. I'd like to thank the dozens of organizations, which contributed photography and information to make *Moving To Charlotte: The Un-Tourist Guide*® such a comprehensive compendium.

Thanks go to Newt Barrett, my publisher. He had the idea for the ***Moving To*** series of books and thought that I was the right person to author the Charlotte edition. Thanks for your confidence in me, Newt.

Thanks to Brant Waldeck of My Creative Team, who produced all the charts in the book and provided some of the photography.

To my lovely bride, Terry, an author in her own right, who tried to keep the grandsons quiet while I was pounding on the keyboard.

Thank you to freelance writers Lauren Blake, Sarah Crosland and Harry Hoover III who greatly improved the book with the sidebar articles they provided. And, finally thanks to Charlotte Chamber CEO Bob Morgan, Foundation for the Carolinas CEO Michael Marsicano and Allen Tate Company President Pat Riley for providing their unique perspectives about my town.

ABOUT THE AUTHOR

Except for a military stint spent in Texas and college in Chapel Hill, Harry Hoover has always lived in Mecklenburg County. His ancestors, the Hoovers came to the area in 1751. His other forebears, the Todds, the Ingles, and the Gaffneys followed closely thereafter.

Harry graduated from West Mecklenburg High School, attended Central Piedmont Community College, and completed his BA at UNC-Chapel Hill. He spent six years as a radio and newspaper journalist, covering cops and courts, hosting a daily call-in talk show, serving as managing editor and performing color commentator duties for UNCC basketball.

He was assistant director of Mecklenburg County Public Service and Information, then worked at a PR firm and an advertising agency, prior to starting his own agency in 2001. He formed marketing agency, My Creative Team, in 2007 and retired from the company in 2016. Harry has gone back to his first love: writing. He has recently published *Born Creative: Free Your Mind, Free Yourself* and is working on new books, writing for online publications, as well as publishing a self-improvement blog, You-Improved.com.

Harry and his wife, Terry, a mystery author, live near Lake Norman where they are often visited by their son, daughter, and grandsons.

CPSIA information can be obtained at www.ICGtesting.com
Printed in the USA
BVIW12n1425110718
521378BV00023B/62